THE
CRASH
TEST BOAT

HOW *YACHTING MONTHLY* **TOOK A 40**FT
YACHT THROUGH 8 DISASTER SCENARIOS

Pete,
Thanks for the
great 'cover quote'!

best wishes
Paul

ADLARD COLES NAUTICAL

B L O O M S B U R Y

LONDON · NEW DELHI · NEW YORK · SYDNEY

CRASH TEST BOAT

Published by Adlard Coles Nautical
an imprint of Bloomsbury Publishing Plc
50 Bedford Square, London WC1B 3DP
www.adlardcoles.com

Material from *Yachting Monthly* magazine © IPC Media Ltd
Additional material © Paul Gelder

First edition published 2013

ISBN: 978-1-4081-5727-5
ePub: 978-1-4081-5920-0
ePDF: 978-1-4081-5923-1

A CIP catalogue record for this book is available from the British Library.

This book is produced using paper that is made from wood grown in managed, sustainable forests. It is natural, renewable and recyclable. The logging and manufacturing processes conform to the environmental regulations of the country of origin.

Typeset in Myriad Pro
Printed and bound in China by C&C Offset Printing Co

Note: while all reasonable care has been taken in the publication of this book, the publisher takes no responsibility for the use of the methods or products described in the book.

CONTENTS

Foreword by Mike Golding

With around half a million miles of racing or sailing behind me, across all the oceans of the world, relying upon the mechanics of complex technical sail boats, nature's general wrath and our own human frailties, I have experienced perhaps more than my fair share of 'Crash Test' type experiences.

We plan every event with care and precision and as a team we spend weeks, even months, during the build-up to major races trying to imagine what would, could or might go wrong. Without exception we work on the basis of 'Plan for the worst, hope for the best'. Unfortunately, and in spite of all our best efforts, things can, will and eventually do still go wrong from time to time.

To date I have not lost a boat– I'm touching wood as I write this, prior to the 2012–2013 Vendée Globe – nor has anyone aboard our boats been seriously injured or gone (far) overboard. Considering the extreme boats and conditions we have experienced, I consider this a tangible success.

But after two serious capsizes (in multihulls), numerous dismastings – two of them deep in the Southern Ocean – a near sinking or two, a broken keel 50 miles from the finish of the 2004-2005 Vendée Globe, medical issues for both myself and others, not to mention the odd fire onboard… I guess I must accept that I am qualified to write the prologue for this book about the Yachting Monthly Crash Test Boat series.

As far as I know this is the first time that a normal cruising type boat has been subjected to this variety of extreme crash tests under relatively controlled conditions. Every road car is tested in this way before it can go on the roads. Boats, however, do not have the same requirements, even though the range of possible disasters is so much wider. Testing and then evaluating those outcomes, provides sailors with the opportunity to learn the results from the comfort of a book, rather than needing to risk life and limb. Such knowledge could have some preventative effect, or may help provide experience that could save lives.

I was asked initially to help with the capsize test. Paul and his team of crash testers did not at any point shy away from tests of catastrophic proportions. When I met the team they seemed to revel in the task of abusing that poor old boat in the pursuit of knowledge.

In the IMOCA class (International Monohull Open Class Association), the 60ft boats that we race in the Vendée Globe, we are obliged to do a full 360° capsize test when the boats are first launched; each year thereafter we must tip the yacht on its side for a 90° stability test, so we are perhaps the most experienced in conducting such extreme tests. On the day of the capsize, it surprised everyone present (including me) just how easy and how little force was needed to get this standard cruising yacht to capsize fully. It will surprise even more people that, like almost all boats, she was very happy to sit there in the marina – upside down but fully stable. Most leisure sailors still think of and refer to their boats as being self-righting – clearly this is not correct.

Perhaps you are thinking 'none of this will ever happen to me'? Perhaps you are careful, skilled and experienced? Possibly the boats you sail are 'safe', so you feel you are not exposed to such dangers. It is also possible that this very act of self-denial may lead you blindly towards an unseen crisis. Certainly, everything I have learned and all of my experience tells me that this is 'wrong thinking'. The question you really have to address is what might happen, and what will I do if and when it does?

Good planning and preparation is the subject for another book. Meanwhile, this book will help you to better understand the causes and effects of some serious eventualities aboard a yacht. The knowledge gained here could equip you to deal with a crisis – helping to ensure that you and your crew are kept safe.

As a former Fire Service Officer, it is perhaps my training above everything else that has provided the ideal background for the uncertainties of my career in high performance professional sailing, where serious problems are often seen as just 'par for the course'. Just like attending a 999 fire emergency, every single incident on a boat is completely unique and requires different actions in response. It is vital you are able to adapt to each scenario and deal with the priorities logically, while always maintaining some level of calm detachment to assess, plan and put into action what needs to be done.

As a professional sailor the ultimate accolade is always to stand on top of the podium. However, I must confess that I derive a significant personal satisfaction from having overcome some of the random crash test dramas featured in this book. Staying calm, never giving up and always holding the safety and well-being of the crew are all at the top of the priorities.

Mike Golding OBE

www.mikegolding.com
@goldingmike

Introduction by Paul Gelder

The Crash Test Boat series is a world-first and certainly exploded a few myths about safety at sea. She's been called 'Britain's most abused boat' – deliberately stranded on a shingle bank, capsized twice through 360 degrees, 'sunk', set ablaze and, finally, blown up in a gas explosion off the Isle of Wight.

In 2010, *Yachting Monthly* magazine acquired a 40ft Jeanneau Sun Fizz ketch, which, over a period of eight months, was tested to destruction. The project has been described as a nautical version of television's *Top Gear* car stunts, though the tests had the added bonus of offering potentially life-saving lessons for sailors. We documented seven of our crash tests in live-action footage too, accompanied by commentary and safety tips from the team. Each clip can be viewed using the QR codes on the chapter opener pages in this book.

No one else has recorded so graphically, in words and pictures, what happens when calamity strikes out of the blue. But it's when things go wrong that we learn our most valuable lessons – and the ethos of the Crash Test Boat series was all about encouraging self-reliance, good seamanship and safety.

Each chapter of accidents in our so-called 'controlled experiments' proved to be a step into the unknown. But as solo sailing legend Chay Blyth once said, 'Without risk there is no adventure…'

In a risk-averse culture, obsessed with 'health and safety', we had our work cut out to comply with a list of regulations and legislation as thick as a telephone directory. We had a duty of care to everyone involved. We also had to convince the authorities – the Marine Coastguard Agency (MCA), the Marine Accident Investigation Branch (MAIB) and our publishers, IPC Media – that our experiments were not reckless stunts.

Before each test, Chris Beeson, the Crash Test Boat skipper, and I had to fill out 'risk assessment' forms, identifying hazards – injury, drowning, boat sinking and pollution – and offer convincing 'control methods'. Risk was measured on a scale from 'low' to 'high', 'extreme' and, of course, 'unacceptable'. The latter saw Chris banned from being aboard the yacht during the capsize test.

Another major hurdle to overcome was the threat of damage to the environment by pollution, especially from the capsize and explosion tests. The MCA cautioned in an email: 'While this [pollution] is accepted when a genuine accident occurs, these are pre-planned test which wouldn't fall under that exception.' Worryingly, they also added the proviso: 'Should the MCA believe at any point that the vessel has become dangerously unsafe we would have to stop that test progressing any further.'

During the capsize test in Ocean Village Marina, I asked Mike Golding, 'What's the worst case scenario?' He replied, 'We lose control and the boat sinks to the bottom of the marina!' The night before, Chris had texted me to say he couldn't extract all the oil from the engine. Luckily, we succeeded on the day.

Only now can it be revealed that during the dismasting test there was a moment when we feared we might black out the Isle of Wight. As the yacht drifted up the Solent, the mast was dragging along the seabed where a 'submarine power cable' from the mainland was marked on the chart!

At one point, I was told that creating a real gas explosion was 'too dangerous and uncontrollable' and we should examine simulating a blast. Who would give us permission to explode a 40ft yacht in what was called 'a crazy experiment'? It was suggested we might have to go offshore, beyond the 12-mile limit – and the reach of the law. David Lanfranchi, a risk management expert consulted by IPC, gave me the phone number of John Richardson, the Oscar-winning special effects legend, who worked on *Alien* and the Harry Potter films. Here was a man who knew how to make a blast. Fortunately, in the nick of time, we found the answer to our plans, thanks to a meeting with Paul Boissier, CEO of the RNLI. Paul is a former Chief Naval Warfare Officer and he put me in touch with Admiral Sir George Zambellas, now Commander-in-Chief Fleet, which led us to 'Harry' Palmer, the Royal Navy's Fleet Explosives Officer.

Our biggest challenge, before we could even begin our test series, was to find a suitable yacht to wreck. I will always be grateful to Robert Holbrook, founder and managing director of Admiral Yacht Insurance, who bravely stepped in to become our project's title sponsor, later writing a cheque to buy a ketch worth some £30,000. A passionate sailor himself – twice voted National Finn champion – Robert, having paid out thousands of pounds in insurance claims to unlucky sailors, recognised the potential of our series to educate yachtsmen.

We had invaluable support from the RYA, the RNLI, who stood by during the explosion, Osmotech UK, one of Europe's leading yacht repair centres, and Marina Developments Limited, who gave us free berthing at Hamble Point Marina. Our expert consultants included solo sailor Mike Golding, Paul Lees from Crusader Sails and Warsash Maritime Academy.

We received accolades from as far away as America and Australia. 'In my 30 years of lecturing and research on yacht and boat design, this must be the most beneficial project for boat safety that I have ever encountered – it certainly deserves a safety award,' wrote Kim Klaka, Safety Officer for Fremantle Sailing Club's cruising section.

In April in 2012, the Crash Test Series won the Innovation of the Year award at IPC Media's Editorial awards.

Looking back over 45 years in journalism, the Crash Test Boat series was one of the most exciting and rewarding 'assignments' of my career, as well as the the most stressful! There were sleepless nights, waking up to scribble 'must do' and 'don't forget' notes. But how many people get to blow-up a 40ft yacht as part of their job – and all in a good cause? As sailor Richard Houghton told me: 'The project has been a fabulous advert for yacht safety and accident prevention.' And IPC Publisher Simon Owen added: 'It's been a remarkable, original piece of journalism that has a lifespan way beyond the magazine issues in which it appeared.'

Paul Gelder

Meet the Crash Test Boat team

MIKE GOLDING

SOLO OCEAN RACER
One of the world's top ocean sailors, awarded an OBE in 2007 for his contribution to the sport of sailing, Mike has sailed singlehanded around the world five times. Once called 'the unluckiest yachtsman in the world', he has been dismasted several times and once lost his keel in the final stage of the famous Vendee Globe round-the-world race – but still managed to cross the finish line.

PAUL LEES

SAILMAKER
Founder and principal of Crusader Sails, in Poole, Dorset, Paul was our consultant on the dismasting and jury rig tests. A veteran of the 1979 Fastnet Race and a former skipper of the J Class yacht, *Velsheda*, he is a highly experienced inshore and offshore racer. He has been sailmaking for more than 40 years also been a boat-builder with 32 boats launched.

PAUL GELDER

***YACHTING MONTHLY* EDITOR (2002–2012)**
No stranger to disaster at sea, Paul has edited the best selling anthology of true-life sailing disasters, *Total Loss*, plus it's companion volume, *Sunk Without Trace* (Adlard Coles Nautical). He was presented with the Ocean Cruising Club's Award of Merit in 2005 for launching a campaign to save Sir Francis Chichester's famous ketch *Gipsy Moth IV*, which sailed around the world on the 40th anniversary of Chichester's epic voyage.

MARTIN LODGE

CONSULTANT ON FIRE TEST
Sub-officer Firefighter Martin Lodge teaches at the International Fire Training Centre, at Warsash Maritime Academy, together with firefighters Andy Baynham and Barry Marsh. Between them they have more than 100 years of fire-fighting experience.

LT CDR MICHAEL ('HARRY') PALMER

EXPLOSIVES CONSULTANT
A keen sailor, Lt Cdr Palmer joined the Royal Navy in 1989 and studied to become a Weapon Engineer. He has served on a variety of frigates and destroyers and in 2000 was selected to study for an MSc in Explosives Ordnance Engineering. As Fleet Explosives Officer he is responsible for the standards of explosives safety in all ships.

JIM HIRST

REPAIR SPECIALIST
We destroyed and 'Jim fixed it!' Jim co-founded Osmotech, the yacht repair specialists, at Hamble Point Marina, Hampshire, with Mike Ingram. Together they took Osmotech from a market leader for osmosis treatment to a global repair and refit centre.

CHRIS BEESON

CRASH TEST BOAT SKIPPER
Chris is *Yachting Monthly's* Assistant Editor and has more than 30 years' sailing experience with 40,000 miles logged, including two westward transatlantic passages three Fastnet Races and one non-stop Round Britain and Ireland Race. He is *Yachting Monthly's* chief boat tester and equipment reviewer and is also author of the Handbook of *Survival at Sea*.

KIERAN FLATT

***YACHTING MONTHLY* EDITOR**
A sailor for more than three decades, Kieran has spent the last 10 years cruising his 28ft sloop, a Twister, around the English Channel, the Bay of Biscay, the Bristol Channel, and the Irish Sea. He has also crewed in offshore races and worked as a sailing instructor in both the UK and France. He was appointed *YM* editor in 2012.

ANDREW BROOK

CRASH TEST BOAT CREW
Joined *Yachting Monthly* on the Geoff Pack Scholarship, launched in memory of its former editor from 1992-1997. Andrew had sailed for 15 years and worked on Mediterranean charter yachts: one season instructing with Sunsail and one season as flotilla engineer with Setsail.

STUART CARRUTHERS

RYA CRUISING MANAGER
With more than 40 years' sailing experience and thousands of sea miles, both as crew and skipper, Stuart was actively involved in our 'Aground!' test and was consulted on other disaster scenarios in the Crash Test Boat series. He has detailed knowledge of many technical and regulatory issues that affect leisure sailors.

DAVID STOPARD

GAS SAFETY CONSULTANT
A registered Gas Safe engineer, David is MD of Marine Systems Engineering Ltd, which specialises in marine LPG systems. A marine engineer, he was formerly senior engineer at Rival Bowman Starlight yachts. A keen sailor, he has logged 100,000 miles, including 10,000 miles singlehanded. He lives on board his Sadler 32, *Capella*.

PAUL STEVENS

CONSULTANT ON 'MAJOR LEAKS' TEST
A founding member of British Marine Surveyors Europe, Paul was the whistleblower for a seacock safety campaign run by *Yachting Monthly* magazine. He was the consultant on our 'Major Leaks!' test. Author of *Surveying Yachts and Small Craft* (Adlard Coles Nautical), Paul is a lecturer at the International Boatbuilding Training College, in Lowestoft, Suffolk.

JERRY HENWOOD

RIGGING CONSULTANT

A lifelong sailor, Jerry runs his own bespoke rigging service from his workshop in Gosport, Hampshire, and was one of our consultants for the dismasting and jury rig test. Every year Admiral Yacht Insurance, the sponsor of the Crash Test Boat series, send Jerry to Las Palmas, in the Canary islands, to check the rigs of yachts taking parting the Atlantic Rally for Cruisers.

SIMON JINKS

CONSULTANT

Simon formerly managed the RYA Yachtmaster programme for sail and motor vessels as well as the RYA navigation and safety courses. He is now a partner in SeaRegs LLP, specialising in the MCA commercial codes of practice, safety management systems and RYA training.

MARK LEES

CREW ON DISMASTING AND JURY RIG

Mark, 19, is a former Optimist dinghy junior national champion, RYA youth national match racing champion and has held many other junior titles. He was also a helmsman in 2011 for the British Keelboat Academy, racing Niklas Zennstrom's Farr 45, *Kolga*.

LESTER MCCARTHY

PHOTOGRAPHER

Lester has more than 40 years' experience with many extended passages around the UK and Europe. He has owned many boats, from a tugboat to a classic wooden Vertue sloop.

GRAHAM SNOOK

PHOTOGRAPHER

Graham is *Yachting Monthly's* staff photographer with more than 32 years' sailing experience and more than 10,000 sea miles logged. He has cruised in the Caribbean, the Indian Ocean and the Mediterranean and owns a Sadler 32 sloop, *Pixie*.

STEVE ADAMS

FILM-MAKER

Steve has 20 years' experience in TV production and now produces programmes for his own website, www.yachtingTV.co.uk, which has featured films on crossing the Atlantic and Bay of Biscay. He is a passionate sailor always looking for adventurous ways to bring sailing to life on TV.

The Crash Test Boat

Our first challenge was to find a suitable yacht to wreck. 'I shall be trying my hardest not to form any emotional connection with this yacht,' said *Fizzical's* new owner, Robert Holbrook, the boss of Admiral Yacht Insurance.

Having signed up to sponsor the Crash Test Boat project at the end of 2010, Robert found *Fizzical*, a 1982 Jeanneau Sun Fizz ketch, at Hamble Point Marina, Hampshire, in December. Well loved and maintained, she seemed too good to destroy, but she was for sale at a knockdown price. Given a 'makeover' she could easily have been sold for around £30,000.

Her co-owners for the past nine years had been David Short (45) and Martin Rolfe (40), both keen yachtsmen and friends for almost 20 years. They were to become enthusiastic followers of the Crash Test series and even attended the gas explosion, when their former pride and joy suffered her final humiliation.

Ironically, they first saw *Fizzical* listed for sale on *Yachting Monthly*'s website ybw.com. She was ashore in a boatyard in Preveza, in the Greek Ionian, having been sailed there from the UK by her previous owner, Mr Melling, from Lancaster, with his family.

'She looked like a lot of boat for the money,' said Martin. 'David and I had chartered several times in Greece which gave us the idea to buy a yacht.' So at the end of 2001, having flown to Athens and driven to Preveza, they wrote a cheque and *Fizzical* was theirs. For the next few years they enjoyed many cruising trips around the Ionian, moving the yacht from to Lefkada Marina and entering the Ionian Regatta

Robert Holbrook, managing director of Admiral Yacht Insurance at the wheel

several times. In 2007 they decided to bring *Fizzical* home to the UK, to make more use of her, before finally to deciding to sell her and buy a Hanse three years later.

'I don't mind what you do to her. I've written her off in my mind,' said new owner Robert, adding, 'but it would be nice if we could all go for a sail before we blow her up!'

Chris (left) chats with Robert in the saloon, amidst the 'doomed symphony in brown'

*Fizzical **under colourful cruising chute***

Robert relaxes in the cockpit with Chris at the wheel

Chris Beeson, the newly appointed Crash Test Boat skipper, together with photographer Lester McCarthy, obliged with a test sail in March, hoisting the yacht's one-year-old suit of Kemp performance cruising sails in a breeze that barely blew out the creases.

Sailed later on in a wet Force 4, with full main and 80 per cent of the genoa, she fetched out at around 8 knots and beam-reached back at 8-9 knots. Though over-pressed in gusts, she never lost her head where a modern cruiser with a wider stern and a single rudder might.

'In the early 1980s she must have seemed quite hairy, but by today's standards the ketch, at least, has a very

modest sail area, observed Chris. 'Yacht design has come an awfully long way since then,' he added, looking down below at the limited light and ventilation. 'The Stygian gloom is overpowering. Her interior would need a complete overhaul to seem anything but dungeonesque, with her cramped cabins,' he ranted. 'Using the forward heads is like shutting yourself in a small, fetid humidor!'

Chris memorably described the accommodation as 'a doomed symphony in brown, with sagging nicotine-yellow vinyl headlining, jaundiced Formica, stressed executive cork tiles in the two heads and mournful ebony-trimmed mahogany veneers dripping gloom throughout.'

Martin Rolfe writes up the day's log at the chart table

Sunset as Fizzical arrives at the Greek island of Kastos

Fizzical under full sail in the Solent

Martin's wife Anna and her brother Tim, re-sealing the saloon window panels in Preveza.

David Short and Martin Rolfe, with gas safety expert Peter Spreadborough (seated), watch as their yacht explodes off the Isle of Wight

Most of the 600 Sun Fizz 40s built between 1980–86 were sloop-rigged, so *Fizzical* was somewhat unusual. However, the Sun Fizz range had sparked a new age of performance cruising and cemented Jeanneau's mass market credentials. The Philippe Briand-design, with its fin and spade appendages, set a new benchmark for performance cruising – Sun Fizz 40s placed second and third in a two-handed Transatlantic Race in 1980. 'She is still recognised as one of the first boats that proved the validity of the performance cruiser concept,' Chris noted.

The yacht boasted 11 berths in total, which seemed wildly excessive, and included two 6ft 2in pilot berths in the saloon. She had a 45hp BMW engine and the hand-laid construction of the hull was very solid for such a light boat, as subsequently proved during the destructive testing.

Despite all her shortcomings when set against modern designs, Chris admitted that the hull is sweetly designed. 'She'll perform as well as many modern cruisers and the price is tempting,' he said, adding: 'Should Robert find himself warming to her, all he needs to do is spend a night on board, after which he'll light the fuse that detonates her himself!'

1 AGROUND

What to do when you run aground

Provided you refloat without any damage, it doesn't much matter how, but the aim of this test was to go step-by-step through the various methods, from simple to increasingly desperate, and assess how effective they are. Armed with the knowledge in this feature, you can react more quickly and more effectively – and on a falling tide it could make the difference between a nuisance and a nightmare.

The nature of the grounding will suggest what type of bottom you've found. Slow deceleration means mud, quicker deceleration means gravel, sharper still is sand and a dead stop is a rock or a wreck. Check charts to confirm but be aware that things can change – as a Yachtmaster Instructor, our consultant Simon Jinks once ran aground on a Ford Capri. If you're grounded on rocks, use only the heeling techniques – don't attempt to turn the yacht because you could rip out the keel.

' If you're grounded on rocks, don't attempt to turn the yacht because you could rip out the keel '

The Crash Test Boat team (left to right): RYA Cruising Manager, Stuart Carruthers, Kieran Flatt, Andrew Brook and Chris Beeson

14 ways to get out of trouble if you run aground

The Crash Test Boat team tried every possible method to discover what worked and what didn't, so if it happens to you, you'll know just what to do

1 First response: change direction immediately

Change direction while you still have way. As a general rule the genoa will haul the bow away from the wind and the main will bring it up so, depending on wind direction, try bearing away, tacking and leaving the jib backed or gybing, to go back down your track, or at least away from shallow water. This will most likely be a series of bumps – heeling, vertical, heeling – as the keel bounces down into deeper water.

Having touched, we tacked, leaving the jib backed

2 Hang off the shrouds to heel the boat

It's generally accepted that you should get all but one crew to hang onto the downwind shrouds to increase heel, which reduces draught on fin and long keel yachts. In reality, however, we found that three stocky gents hanging onto the shrouds had little effect on the heel of the 40ft Crash Test Boat and, as a first response, backing the genoa (on a windward shore) was much more effective if there was any sort of sailing breeze. That said, with a smaller crew on a smaller yacht, it might just make the difference you need if you react as soon as you run aground. In light winds it's worth trying to heel her both ways. If you're fore-and-aft along the contour, heeling the mast offshore reduces draught and heeling it inshore means the keel may slide down into deeper water. Remember to furl the jib if it's countering your heel.

Weight forward reduces draught on bilge and long keelers

Conversely, if you have twin keels and you've been sailing upwind, reducing heel will also reduce draught, so drop the main, furl away most of the jib and back what's left. Another trick on long and twin keelers is to move any spare crew to the bow, which also reduces draught. This method is the only one available for skippers of wing-keeled boats as heeling will dig the wing tips into the bottom.

On the 40ft Crash Test Boat, three 'heavies' on the shrouds didn't induce much heel

3 Start the engine and try to motor off

If your first response doesn't work, check there are no lines over the side and start the engine. On a lee shore, drop sail, otherwise use canvas and crew to generate as much heel as possible. Select astern and give her plenty of throttle. If that doesn't work, select forward and try turning hard to port then hard to starboard. This might loosen the mud's suction on the keel or dig a hole in the shingle, allowing you to break free by selecting hard astern again. You'll be stirring up the bottom a fair bit so make regular checks of the raw water strainer. After several hours of testing, ours remained clear.

If that doesn't work, get everyone into lifejackets and switch them to manual if possible. In the next few minutes you'll be jumping all over the boat so the chances of ending up in the water are heightened. It may be shallow enough that drowning won't be a problem but you could be swept away by current and the lifejacket will keep you afloat long enough to be retrieved.

You'll churn up plenty of sediment so check the engine's raw water strainer regularly

4 Put the crew on the boom end

Now get all but one crew out to the end of the boom to increase the heel generated by the backed genoa. Drop the main and check the gooseneck fitting. Secure the main halyard around the boom end to support the topping lift so that the crew weight is not supported by a single shackle or casting, run the lazyjacks forward to the mast, release the mainsheet and rig a foreguy from the boom end to the forward cleat to haul the boom outboard. Leave the engine running and get your crew to shimmy out onto the boom end while you try to reverse off. Again, we found this made little difference to the heel of our boat but react quick enough and a little difference is all you need.

Throttle astern, then forward, left rudder and right to dig her free – unless you're aground on rock

❛ *Select astern and give her plenty of throttle. If that doesn't work, select forward and try turning hard to port then hard to starboard* **❜**

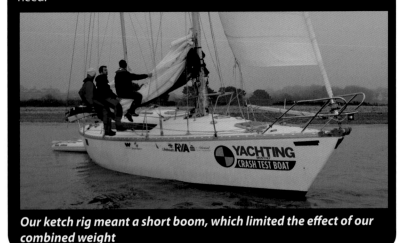

Our ketch rig meant a short boom, which limited the effect of our combined weight

Double check your position on the chart

First, use a leadline at the bow to find out where deeper water lies

> ' *The worst case scenario is running aground at HW Springs. You could be there for two weeks* '

5 Check position and tide, survey depths

If you're still not free, drop all sail, lift the cabin sole, check for leaks and make sure the keelbolts are secure. Next, shut the stable door by checking your position on a chart to find out what the bottom is and where deeper water lies. Also check the tide. If it's rising, just wait for 20 minutes or so. If it's falling, keep trying to haul yourself off. If you can't, you have up to six hours to learn your lesson. The worst case scenario is running aground at HW Springs. You could be there for two weeks.

Before setting any ground tackle, check for deeper water using a leadline – it needn't be more complicated than a shackle on a length of knotted string – poled out using a boathook either side of the bow, beam and stern. If you don't learn anything from that, launch the tender and leadline further afield to establish where the deeper water lies. While we were leadlining, the line would often be taken by the current so try moving with the current to get an accurate reading.

If using a lead line doesn't reveal anything, launch the tender

6 Make sure you don't go further aground

Next, deploy the bower anchor in deeper water and deploy the kedge back down your track. On a lee shore in a rising wind, if you've tried all the above, securing position is your No1 priority – get the anchor and kedge dug in under deeper water and get both cables tight. Rig a trip line for the kedge because it's likely you'll need to retrieve and reset it.

Andrew was volunteered to handle the groundtackle and found the job fairly easy, but then he's 24 years old, 6ft-plus and beefy. Stuart noted that most cruising yacht owners won't fit that description and that dropping and resetting groundtackle by hand would represent a real challenge for most. It's a fair point. The aim here is to test every possible method but only you can decide what works for you.

Having located deeper water, we used the tender to set the anchor and kedge. We were concerned about putting a hefty CQR and 30m of 12mm chain in our tender, half expecting the load to turn it into a rubber ring, but as we loosened the windlass clutch and

gently fed out the chain, our borrowed Tetra Boats tender didn't flinch. By securing the tender to the yacht's bow, we limited relative movement, making loading safer.

We shackled the anchor to the tender's cleat and towed it in the water because it made launching much easier than heaving it overboard. If you have an electric windlass, give the throttle some revs in neutral and haul the cable tight to make sure the anchor's set and that the chain hasn't piled up on top of it. Without a windlass, hitch a line to the chain, or lead the cable aft, to a winch and get some tension in the cable.

In his book *A Sea Vagabond's World*, Bernard Moitessier explained how he hauled his yacht off a lee shore by dropping the anchor then diving down repeatedly and walking the anchor further and further out into deeper water before hauling her off with the windlass. I tried it once in Greece and it can be done, but there are two things to

consider: the method may work well in the clear, sandy-bottomed South Pacific, but it's not so good in muddy Southampton Water. Plus, using a dinghy is much quicker.

Marlow Ropes supplied us with 30m of 12mm multibraid (worth £94) to use as a kedge line and I would highly recommend having that length of cordage on board. As a kedge line it was invaluable in our test but it also means you have spare sheets and halyards if ever you need them. As any good chandler will tell you, 'better to look at it than look for it.'

We launched the Fortress kedge, fitted with a trip line, in the same way and ran its cable through a fairlead onto a primary winch, then wound until it was tight. Maintaining as much heel as possible and having loosened the bower anchor cable, we tried to winch her back down her track but the keel was too deep in the mud by then. We expected the kedge to trip but it gripped the mud admirably.

1. Secure the tender to the yacht to make loading safer

2. The windlass clutch controls the chain. It's fine to pile up the chain in the dinghy

3. Andrew heads off to deploy the anchor

4. Pay out the chain before setting the anchor in deep water

5. The bower anchor protects your position and the kedge would help you haul yourself back down the track

7 Lighten the yacht to reduce draught

Next we tried another method of reducing draught. We loaded the tender with anything heavy – liferaft, toolkit, outboard, jerry cans, mooring warps, spare sails, etc – emptied the water tanks then tried to motor off again while winding on the kedge line. Then we moved the loaded tender round to the offshore side, attached the main halyard to the boom end and rigged a foreguy as before, rigged a bridle for lifting the tender, and ran the lifting line through a block on the boom end, then a jib car and back to a primary winch. The lifting line chafed on the lifelines so a block on the toerail would be a better choice. The bridle's knot was soon up against the block so we lowered the tender, released the vang and mainsheet, hoisted the boom on topping lift and main halyard and lifted the tender again. This was one of the more effective methods of simultaneously reducing draught and inducing heel but make sure your bridle is up to it – you don't want to lose the tender's contents.

Emptying water tanks lowers displacement and reduces draught

> ❛ *This was one of the more effective methods of simultaneously reducing draught and inducing heel but make sure your bridle is up to it* ❜

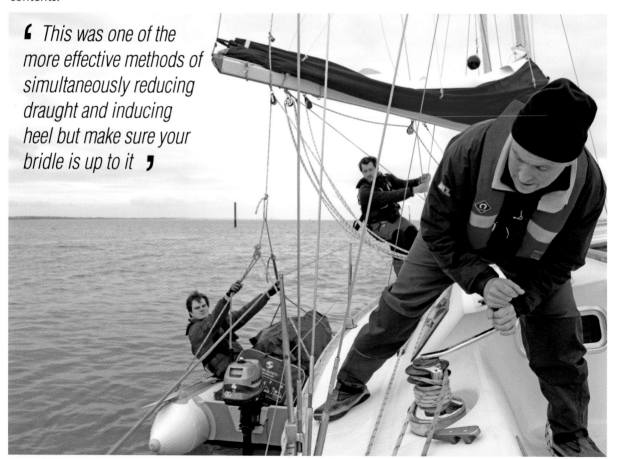

The bridle knot soon met the boom end block so we raised the boom and tried again

8 Use the kedge anchor to winch her off

Winching the kedge line through a block up the mast was very effective

Clip the main halyard to a loop of line, attach a block, run the kedge line through it

Using the tender, re-deploy the kedge anchor in deeper water off the offshore beam. Run the cable through the forward fairlead and back to a primary winch and start grinding. This should haul the bow round towards deeper water, which gives the bower anchor cable a fair lead and brings the windlass into play. This will stress the keel root so send someone below to keep an eye on the keelbolts. If the wind is offshore, remember to keep the genoa backed and use the crew to heel. Many of these methods can be used simultaneously.

With the kedge well set in deeper water, we tried to increase heel by improving leverage using the mast height. If you have a spinnaker halyard with a swivelling block, tie a loop in its end, attach a block and run the kedge cable through it, down to a genoa car and back to a primary winch. With plenty of slack in the cable, haul the halyard up the mast and start grinding the winch. In our experience this was easily the most effective method of generating heel.

If you don't have a spinnaker halyard, this method isn't suitable because the halyard is likely to jump out of its sheave. Instead, as we've done here, make a loop in a length of spare line, fasten a block to the loop and

' Haul the halyard up the mast and start grinding the winch. In our experience this was easily the most effective method of generating heel '

tie it around the mast. Then attach a main or genoa halyard, depending on whether the kedge lies fore or aft of the shrouds, rig a downhaul on the loop, run the kedge cable through the block and, with plenty of slack in the cable, haul it up to the first spreaders. Run the cable down from the block, through a genoa car and onto a primary winch, then winch the kedge cable to induce more heel, simultaneously using the engine to drive her off.

You could try using the masthead tow technique with the tender to improve leverage, but we didn't because it bristled with risk. First you would need to run the tender astern – to run forward instead could lift the prop clear of the water – and risk swamping the tender. Second, you would need to rig a quick release on the halyard because if you can haul the boat free and the mast becomes vertical, you could end up with a tender for a burgee.

With throttle on and crew out, some wake might be all you need

If that doesn't work, pass a spinnaker halyard to your new best friend

9 Ever been pleased to see a motorboat?

Ever been pleased to see a motorboat? You will be now. Keep an eye out for any and ask them to motor around you, using the wake to lift you off while you motor astern. As keen for company as you may be, don't get them stranded too. With our keel sunk 0.5m in the mud, there was only 1m of water around us and Lester McCarthy, our photographer, had to trim the powerful outboard engine on his dory to keep the propeller clear of the bottom.

If creating a wake doesn't work, attach a tow line to the bow – make sure it's your line to avoid any potential salvage issues – then very gently try to haul the bow around towards deeper water. Again, this will stress the keel root, so keep a close eye on the keelbolts and release the tow line if there are any signs of failure. Then rig a bridle and ask to be towed off. If you have a spinnaker halyard, you could also try a masthead tow but make it very clear again that the motorboat's throttle must be used gently and cut completely if you can motor free. In sand, another option is to attach bow and stern lines to the powerboat and have her motor gently ahead, using propwash to clear sand from around the keel allowing you to float free.

The masthead tow is effective but it requires kid gloves and concentration

10 Still stuck? Let everyone know

If none of the above has worked, you're clearly well on and will remain so until the tide refloats you. Call the Coastguard on your VHF radio to notify them of your predicament. They will want to know whether you are safe, how many crew are on board and to establish a working channel. If you are stranded on a rocky bottom, make sure they are aware that you will need to abandon if a rock pierces the hull. If you see any powered traffic, hail them on Ch16, or bridge-to-bridge Ch13, and ask them to slow down as their wake will bounce you on the bottom.

' If you see any powered traffic, hail them on Ch16, or bridge-to-bridge Ch13, and ask them to slow down as their wake will bounce you on the bottom '

Regarding day signals and night lights, we couldn't find a vessel aground day signal – three black balls – on sale anywhere so Graham bought three 99p footballs from a supermarket and wrapped them in gaffer tape. For the two all-round reds we needed at night, we bought two sets of emergency nav lights and used the red port lights.

If you're stuck for a tide, notify the coastguard and see if you can make the right day signal

Our DIY day signal for vessel aground was made from three 99p footballs

OCEAN SAFETY · Lifeboats · **RYA** · *Admiral* BOAT INSURANCE · **YACHTING** MONTHLY

11 Make sure she leans uphill

On a lee shore, the bower anchor should be set in deeper water to prevent you being washed up the beach when the tide rises. Now you need to prepare for beaching. Having established where deeper water lies, haul her over so the mast lies towards the shallows. If you don't, your mast could be horizontal or below, and downflooding becomes a real issue when the tide returns.

We dropped our kedge and bower anchor on the sand bar to guarantee we didn't topple downhill. Then we used the elevated kedge line, hauled through a block attached to the spinnaker halyard and back to a winch through the genoa car.

Once she's heeling the right way, you'll need to find ways to protect the hull topsides

' Haul the boat over so the mast lies towards the shallows, or downflooding could become a real issue when the tide returns '

With the kedge set on the spit, Stuart prepares to winch the yacht over at an angle

12 Protect the hull at points of impact

You need to protect the side of the hull when it comes into contact with the bottom. I had planned to fill a sailbag with our largely deflated fenders and haul it into place with lines under the bow and stern but I hugely underestimated their buoyancy – our well-built consultant Stuart Carruthers was standing on the bag and it refused to submerge – and friction on the lines under the hull meant we couldn't haul it into place. This is the RYA's recommended method of protecting the hull but, as Stuart noted, it doesn't work. Finally, we tried to protect the hull with bunk cushions but it was too late – the gap closes remarkably quickly. We ended up with soggy foam cushions that weighed a ton and were still wet two weeks later. Also, as Stuart pointed out, had the boat been owned by one of us, the adrenalin would have been pumping and we'd have had no qualms about getting a bootful and stuffing something – anything – between the hull and the bottom.

We put our partially deflated fenders into a bag, ready to protect the hull

We decided that our board-backed saloon seating would have offered the best protection, or the heads door stuffed into a sleeping bag. For a hypothetical grounding on rocks we considered shoving a partially deflated tender bow-first into the gap, hauling the painter under the hull, and re-inflating the tender. After our experience with the fenders, a more realistic choice seemed something board-backed which wasn't buoyant.

Our final attempt ended up with wet, heavy cushions and no hull protection

Friction and buoyancy stopped us immersing the bag under the hull

13 Seal all hatches, lockers and through-hulls

Next, secure all hatches and cockpit lockers, cover your coachroof ports with storm boards if you have them. Remember that when heeled the exhaust and heads swan necks may no longer work and could possibly allow water to run back into the engine or hull. If you're drying on the same side as the exhaust, consider some means of stopping water entering the exhaust outlet and close all seacocks. You should also use duct tape to seal the fuel breather and heater outlets as required. While you're dried out, check the rudder and keel root, as both may have sustained damage. Lift the saloon sole to check the keelbolts. Empty hull lockers and remove saloon seating to expose as much of the downhill side of the hull as you can – if the hull does crack, you need to know about it.

Rudder and keel may have sustained damage. Check them while you can

Check keelbolts and empty 'downhill' lockers to inspect the hull

14

Settle down and prepare to be uncomfortable

Now you can settle down below, shutting the washboards behind you, and prepare for a very uncomfortable few hours at an angle that makes everything difficult. It was both unnerving and exhausting moving around on deck and below at 45 degrees – the galley was unusable – so I found a berth and slept for an hour. In stronger conditions, or on a lee shore, grab the hand-held VHF radio, shut the washboards behind you, carry the tender ashore and wait for the tide to return. Notify the Coastguard that the crew is no longer on board. Perhaps you can phone a powerboat-owning friend and ask for help when you're buoyant again.

Once she's refloated, use the methods described above to get yourself off. You may have sucked lot of debris into the engine water intake, driving the prop around and scouring the bottom. You have plenty of time to clean it, otherwise you may end up on the putty again... Drying out will drain water away from the engine intake so you may need to bleed the system with water through the strainer.

> *It was both unnerving and exhausting moving around on deck and below at 45 degrees – the galley was unusable*

Accept your limitations

We wanted to try every method we could think of to refloat so we were fairly exhaustive in our approach. By the end, we were fairly exhausted too – and there were at least three of us onboard. Heaving a big Bruce anchor and thirty metres of chain about, emptying lockers and piling their contents into a tender, and grinding remorselessly on primary winches is not within the physical scope of every cruising couple. Don't forget that in most circumstances you can call for help. If you do end up drying out, don't underestimate the difficulty of moving around at a 45 degree angle. It's exhausting and, if the cabin sole is wet, fairly dangerous too. If you don't feel up to it, get off the boat and into the tender if weather permits, or call for assistance and ask to be taken ashore. Better still, don't run aground in the first place.

Manhandling liferafts, fuel tanks, anchors and kedges imposes a big physical toll

How to avoid grounding

2 Look out for patches of short, breaking chop, and lighter or discoloured water – it could be a tide line but it could be shallows. You may also sense a general change in the boat's motion.

1 If sailing over unavoidable shallow water on your passage, make sure it's on a rising tide and start early. Running aground is usually OK if it is slow, soft and with plenty of tidal rise left.

4 In shallow water, sail the boat upright unless she is a bilge keeler, in which case her draught may be greater when she's heeled over than on an even keel.

3 Don't sail too fast and know exactly where you are, using the GPS and the Mk1 eyeball, and what's around you.

5 Use charts, tide tables and your sounder when sailing in unfamiliar waters.

6 If sailing in a channel, keep to the windward side so if you do touch, you can just back the jib and put the bow down.

How we did it

We conducted our first test on the eastern bank at the mouth of the Hamble River. Unsurprisingly, it was actually very difficult to stay aground on a windward shore with a rising tide. Then the wind rose beyond our abandon limit of 16 knots true, so we called it off.

Our second test, slightly bolder, was conducted with 1m of tidal fall left, at the mouth of Ashlett Creek on Southampton Water, another windward shore. As well as trying various methods of refloating, we were hoping to get some shots of the boat heeled over but in fact the keel sank half a metre into mud, making it difficult to induce heel. The third test, on the western bank at the mouth of the Hamble River, involved running her aground with 2.5m of fall, drying her out and refloating safely.

Before testing, we checked weather, tides and atmospheric pressure – each 10mb above standard pressure, 1013mb, lowers tidal height by 0.1m. We informed Hamble Harbourmaster, Solent Coastguard and Southampton VTS (Vessel Traffic Services) before each test, to avoid any false alarms.

> ❝ It was actually very difficult to stay aground on a windward shore with a rising tide ❞

Our first test took place on a rising tide and we had trouble trying to stay aground. All photo credits: Paul Gelder

We were hard aground in our second test, with the keel stuck in 0.5m of mud

Our final test was drying out. We knew exactly when we would go aground and when we'd refloat

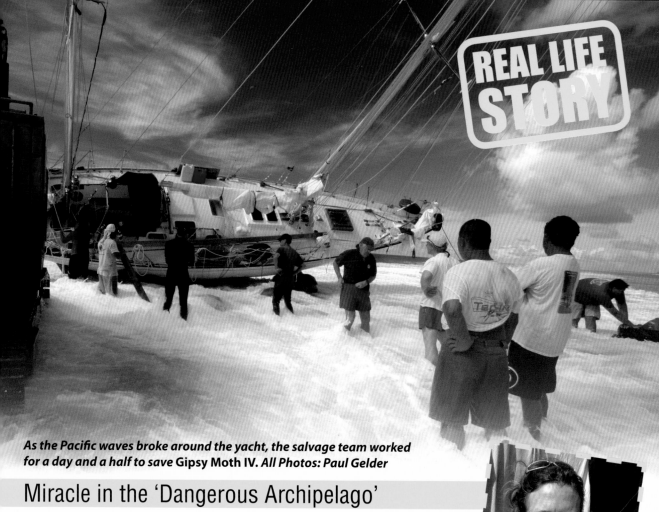

REAL LIFE STORY

As the Pacific waves broke around the yacht, the salvage team worked for a day and a half to save Gipsy Moth IV. All Photos: Paul Gelder

Miracle in the 'Dangerous Archipelago'

Running aground is the most common yachting accident of those featured in this book. Faulty navigation is frequently to blame. But quick thinking and seamanlike preparation can save the day. You might be lucky enough to have soft landing in mud with a rising tide. But it could be a lee shore with hard sand, isolated rocks or a reef. If pounding doesn't destroy your yacht, will she fill with water when the tide returns?

Gipsy Moth IV was 40 degrees off course when she was picked up by a wave and carried onto a reef in the South Pacific in May 2006. This may be a sailor's paradise, but lurking in these exotic blue waters are treacherous reefs waiting to test the most experienced yachtsman.

'It wasn't a huge bang, but as soon as I came on deck I could see she was heeling right over. We were in shallows,' said skipper Antonia Nicholson, a Yachtmaster Ocean Instructor. It was 1815 hours and dark, with no moon or stars, so they couldn't see land beyond. Then they noticed a bright flashing white light in the distance. It was Mota Maherehonae lighthouse, a 92ft-tall square white masonry tower marking the end of the reef which surrounds the

'I wept when I saw the state of Gipsy Moth,' said skipper Antonia Nicholson

The island's only JCB excavator was used to lift the boat so sandbags could be placed underneath and repairs made.

island of Rangiroa like a deadly necklace. The light, flashing every five seconds, had a 20-mile range, but it had been hidden behind the headsail. *Gipsy Moth* had struck the largest atoll in the Tuamotus, notoriously known as 'the Dangerous Archipelago'.

At a subsequent inquiry, it was stated that 'although a lat and long position was taken from the GPS before the incident and written in the log, it was not plotted on the chart.' The last plot had been two hours earlier. The passage plan constructed by the skipper and the mate, which gave a two-mile offing from the reef, was considered to have been ill-conceived, particularly given the navigational challenges of the area and the approach of darkness. A change in helm after 1800 may have resulted in an exacerbation of the course error. The skipper and the mate, who were both below at the time, did not supervise this change in helm and the yacht continued towards the reef.

The waves spun the yacht 180° and her headsail pinned her onto the reef. 'It didn't seem that violent, but the boat continued lurching,' added Antonia. As she exclaimed: 'God, what's going to happen?' a shout of 'Fire!' came from down below. The boat's Primus stove was at such an angle it had burst into flames. Once it was extinguished, Antonia ordered the crew to put on lifejackets. In the chaos down below, the cabin floor was at an angle of 45°.

A Mayday was sent by SSB radio but there was only a weak signal with no response. Parachute flares were set off and seen by other yachts in the area. *Gipsy Moth*'s owners, the UKSA, in Cowes, were called on the Iridium satellite phone. The reef was too isolated and dangerous for rescue that night. Breaking waves on the ocean side made it impossible for two boats to get near the stricken hull. The equivalent of the RNLI in these islands was the Deputy Mayor, a policeman and some fishermen in boats.

UKSA skipper Richard Baggett inspects the keel

The reef was so flat, you could drive a car along it – if it was amphibious!

Skipper Antonia bravely stayed aboard *Gipsy Moth* that first night to guard against possible looters. First, she made sure the crew, including two teenagers, were safely led ashore by first mate Chris Bruce, using a safety line from the boat. They reached a lagoon where rescuers met them in the same fishing boat that had approached from seaward, and took them to safety.

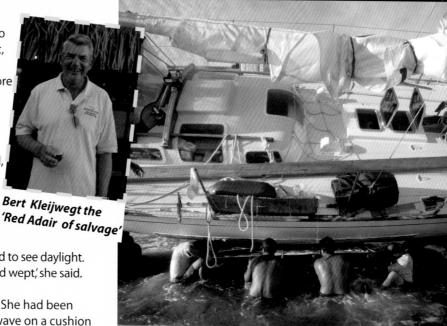

Bert Kleijwegt the 'Red Adair of salvage'

Antonia huddled in the companionway until drawn broke, drenched by waves breaking over the cockpit, 'I have never been so glad to see daylight. Then I saw the state of *Gipsy Moth* and wept,' she said.

It was a miracle the yacht survived. She had been picked up and then dropped by a wave on a cushion of water, as if by the hand of God, mercifully far away enough from the edge of the reef and the pounding surf that would have certainly have smashed her cold-moulded hull to matchwood. The reef was a flat shelf that stretched as far as the eye could see. You could drive a car along – if it was amphibious. Just as with the Crash Test Boat, anchors were laid in a bid to stop the yacht moving.

It was now a race against time to save Sir Francis Chichester's famous 53ft ketch from destruction of the weather worsened. A tsunami warning two days later mercifully turned into a false alarm. A 24-hour incident room was set at the UK Sailing Academy HQ in Cowes and a salvage team met in Tahiti, headed by a man known as 'the Red Adair of salvage', Bert Kleijwegt, who flew in from the world-famous Dutch company Smit, in Rotterdam. Others included a local French marine surveyor, Bruno Videau, Peter Seymour, of Blue Water Rallies, and Richard Baggett, the UKSA's lead skipper, who flew from the UK.

The plan was simple. It had to be. The remote Tuomotu islands have only basic facilities. But at least

'If one big wave had moved the yacht the salvage workers could have been crushed as they nailed plywood patches over the holes'

Working perilously under the keel plywood patches covered an area 2.5m long by a metre high above and below the waterline

A trysail was readied to cover any further damage when the boat was dragged off the reef

Rangiroa had a JCB-type excavator, which was put on a barge and sent 20 miles across the lagoon to the remote wreck location. *Gipsy Moth* was a forlorn sight, lying on the barren reef, her red ensign fluttering from the mizzen mast. The JCB was used to lift the yacht with strops so that sandbags and tyres could be put under the hull to raise the damaged area above water.

Once high enough, workmen crawled underneath to assess the damaged area – some 2.5m long and a metre high. Two big plywood patches coated in Sikaflex sealant were nailed and screwed to the hull. It was difficult, dangerous work, as waves crashed across the reef and workers struggled in chest-high water. Had the yacht moved, they could have been crushed. Another big plywood patch was placed over the others – a sort of giant 'band-aid'. But by now it was dark.

Early next morning, planks of wood were nailed to the hull as a kind of sacrificial sledge on which the yacht could be pulled across the reef to deep water. Quick-setting cement was poured into the damaged hull area from inside the hull and an orange trysail was lashed to the sidedeck, with a line under the hull, ready to deploy in an emergency if the hull was further damaged and leaks needed to be covered. A port authority tug arrived from Tahiti, some 200 miles away. The breaking surf made it impossible to board *Gipsy Moth* after she was dragged off the reef. And if she did leak, who would pump her out? It was decided that Richard Baggett and John Jeffrey would be aboard as she was pulled off. A second boat was stationed off the reef with a high-powered pump, in case it was needed. Two divers were employed in case any stray tow lines fouled the tug's own propeller. This was where Bert's expertise and foresight into the worst case scenario came into play. If necessary, the yacht's liferafts would be used for floatation.

For the first time in six days since the grounding, *Gipsy Moth* started to edge back towards the ocean. A ghastly screeching sound of wood (the sacrificial planks) grinding on coral could be heard over the pounding surf as she was dragged round so her bows faced the edge of the reef. As a big wave broke around her, a final pull slid her into the deep blue Pacific. After six days on the reef, her mast sprang upright to loud cheers from the salvage team. We all embraced in relief.

John Jeffrey later told me, 'Despite a lifetime of military flying, I don't recall many occasions when I have felt more tense. Although we were wearing lifejackets, we did not clip on. If she was going to sink, we wanted to be able to get clear, fast!'

The tug arrives from Tahiti and the tow line is connected to a bridle made from crane strops

Within minutes a radio call from Richard on *Gipsy Moth IV* confirmed that there were no serious leaks. At that moment, 1240 local time on 5 May, *Gipsy Moth IV* was granted a reprieve. The cost of the operation, including the tow, was estimated to be £100,000.

The heart-stopping moment when Gipsy Moth *was dragged over the edge of the reef*

Pounded to destruction

Another grounding incident which offers a frightening reminder of the power of waves was experienced by Robin Gardiner-Hall sailing *Pentina II*, a 33ft yacht, singlehanded to the Baltic in 1979. Like many accidents it had small beginnings. The skipper was trying to lower the main on a dead run but a loose screw in the mainsail track left him effectively hove-to on starboard slowly fore-reaching. He gybed but nearby shipping left him struggling with the stuck main for too long and he ran aground on the edge of the Scharhorn Riff, near the island of Neuwerk, in the mouth of the River Elbe.

He immediately laid out his 35lb CQR anchor and 120ft of chain. As the yacht refloated the chain began snatching violently and sheared the port samson post at deck level. With difficulty he re-secured the chain to the starboard samson post, but 30 minutes later, heavy surf and pounding sheared the second samson post and the chain ran out, ripping out the bitter-end lashing in the chain locker. Distress flares failed to bring help until, finally, he flashed SOS with his torch and was rescued at dawn by a lifeboat. He was later told that flares should always be let off in pairs, at an interval of about 10 seconds, in case someone assumes the first was imagined. Having a secure lashing on the anchor chain's bitter end was also a lesson learned.

Extract from Gipsy Moth IV: A Legend Sails Again, *by Paul Gelder (Wiley Nautical)*

2 CAPSIZE

What happens in a capsize?

Our test involved two separate 360° rollovers. One showed the devastation caused in an unsecured yacht, with no modifications made to counter the effects of loose items flying around. In the second, we secured as much as we could down below, including the galley stove, lockers, chart table, cabin sole, etc.

Since I couldn't be onboard, we needed some other way of finding out what happens when a boat capsizes. Our film-maker for the Crash Test Boat series, Yachting TV's Steve Adams, strategically positioned two waterproof HD cameras below. He also fitted battery lights. With no domestic power and the boat upside-down, there would be very little light in the saloon and we needed to capture the action clearly. The results revealed on his film are frightening.

> ❝ *The dangers were judged to be too great by risk assessment experts and insurers* ❞

To illustrate what would happen to crew down below during a capsize, we bought three mannequins, named Tom, Dick and Harry, and stood one in the galley, laid another in a pilot berth and a third in the forepeak, supposedly out of harm's way.

Harry gets dressed for his uncomfortable berth in the forepeak

UNSECURED ROLL - Without any safety measures taken, she was just an avaerage yacht. How would she cope in a capsize?

SECURED ROLL - What difference would our simple, cheap safety modifications make on deck and below?

Unsecured capsize

Two waterproof cameras filmed the capsizes. The results are frightening

The crane's boom was extended to haul the Crash Test Boat 30ft clear of the pontoon at Ocean Village Marina, and with two Crash Boat crew loosely holding onto the bow and stern lines, the crane operator began to raise the stops and begin the capsize. Soon crashes could be heard from inside the boat.

Once she reached her angle of vanishing stability, around 130°, gravity took over and she rolled over onto her deck. Unnervingly, and rather surprisingly, she was extremely stable upside-down and would never have righted without the crane. After remaining completely inverted for a few seconds, the lift resumed. With the keel 40-45° below vertical, gravity took over again and the keel plunged into the water, sending a mini-tidal wave across the marina.

On the foredeck, the anchor had stayed put, tied into the bow roller, but the chain had broken out of the anchor locker. Fortunately, only a couple of feet dangled over the side because the taut chain between the anchor and the windlass had blocked the bulk of it escaping.

' *Unnervingly, and rather surprisingly, she was extremely stable upside-down and would never have righted without the crane* **'**

As the crane hauled her over, ominous crashes hinted at the imminent chaos within...

Once the keel reached around 40° from vertical, gravity took over and she slammed down dramatically

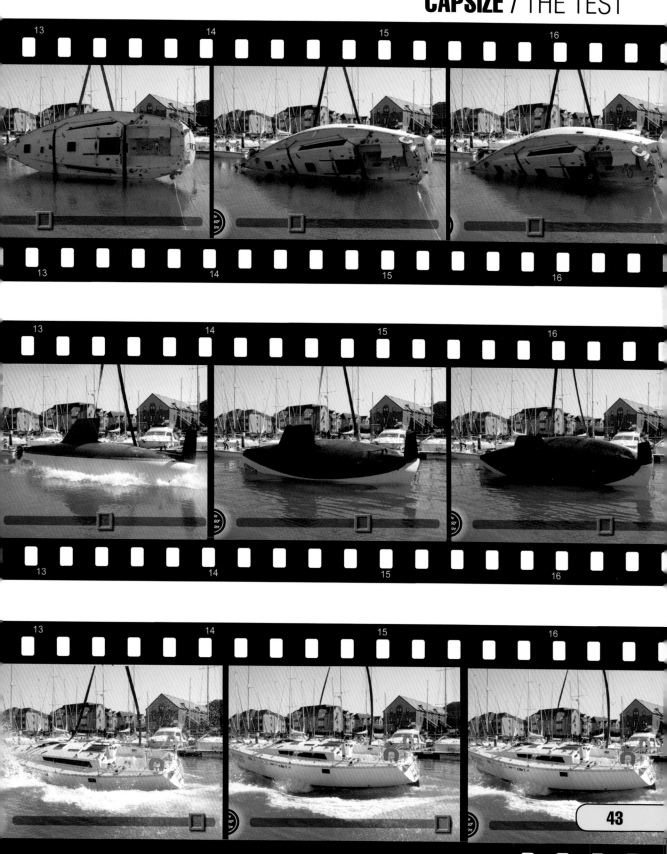

Stepping on deck, I opened the forehatch and stepped into a scene of chaos. The forepeak mannequin, Harry, had broken at the waist and his arm had broken off, too. I was shocked by the violence of the capsize in such a small, safe cabin. It was also obvious that an amazing amount of water had flooded into the boat, something later confirmed by the video. It was still dripping off the headlining, which was soaked throughout. The obvious inlets were the two vents just forward of the mast and the gaps between the hatch, washboards and the companionway, but there could have been others.

In the saloon pilot berth, Dick's lee strap had held him in place but his repose was completely at odds with the devastation surrounding him. The heavy marine ply sole boards had broken free and a small board had lodged under a saloon hand-hold in the deckhead. The starboard leaf had been torn from the saloon table, presumably by the flying sole board. Bilge water was above sole level and debris of every kind floated in it or sank beneath it. Cutlery and spares drawers, though still closed, were full of water. Everything was everywhere. The contents of the stove and coolbox were strewn around the saloon and the aft heads. Both toilets were full. Papier maché charts decorated the galley and the stove had escaped its mounts but thankfully not its well.

Stepping carefully around the carnage, I noticed a steady stream of water running from the engine bay into the heads. A minute later the stream was just as bad. Were we sinking? Though stunned by the wreckage of what, a moment ago, was a tidy boat, the thought that we would founder in the marina focused my mind. Clearly we hadn't hit anything, but had the lifting strop damaged the stern tube? Was the rudder stock damaged when the blade hit the water? The leak was coming from somewhere.

In seconds, everything was scattered everywhere

1979 Fastnet Race skippers reported cockpit lockers were a significant entry point for water in knockdowns

The chain broke through the anchor locker but the anchor, tied in place, stayed put

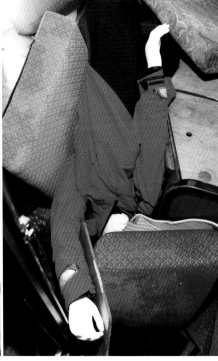

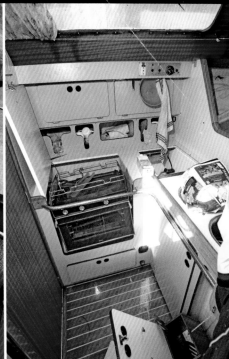

Heavy sole boards in flight would certainly have injured crew below

Harry had broken at the waist and his arm had broken off, too

Only the gas pipe prevented the stove flying across the saloon

' *I was shocked by the violence of the capsize in such a small, safe cabin* '

Using a plastic bowl found wedged under the galley trim, a boot and a glass, three of us started bailing water into the galley sinks – the cockpit drain was blocked. A fourth person looked for the source of the leak. After checking the steering quadrant and finding nothing wrong, we lifted the companionway steps and pointed a torch into the black space behind the engine. There it was – a steady stream of water, thankfully not coming from the stern tube.

Film shot inside the saloon shows water flooding through vents and the companionway

Leaving three bailing, I checked the starboard aft cockpit locker and found it full of water, scooped up during the capsize. Without padlocks, the hasps had just fallen open. The violence of the righting had torn one of the three hinges free and water was now draining from the locker into the engine bay. After struggling to comprehend that the boat's watertightness was so fundamentally undermined, the general sensation was relief. Later, looking at the 1979 Fastnet Race Inquiry, it revealed that 46 of the skippers, 20 per cent of the inquiry's respondents, reported the cockpit lockers were 'a significant water entry point'.
How can we make a boat safer? On the next pages we look at a few simple adjustments we made with basic tools to demonstrate what happens when a secure boat suffers a capsize.

SALOON AND GALLEY

The Crash Test Boat has finger-operated levers as locker latches throughout. We decided these were independent of gravity and secure enough

String, net and a bolt keep plates, fridge contents and stove in place

not to warrant any modification. We thought something might knock the lever from inside the locker but, as no one was onboard, it would be a revealing exercise.

The crockery in the galley was stored in T-slots and these clearly were not gravity-proof. We ran a line through some netting, tied loops in each end and hooked them on to picture hooks nailed into the Formica. Again this was a pretty poor effort aesthetically but it was a quick, cheap solution. How effective would it be?

The yacht's stove has a hinged cover so all we needed to do was fit it with a sliding bolt latch. We thought this, combined with the stove grabrail, should hold the stove in place when it fell out of its mounts. Without a cover, brackets screwed into the stove well, just above the gimbals, should keep it in place. The coolbox lid removed completely so we fastened that with string looped over two screws. Another hasty but hopefully effective solution.

Basic modifications: how to make your boat safer

TANKAGE

The Crash Boat's stainless steel tanks were all laminated into place so, other than emptying them, no preparation was needed. We couldn't find a way of getting to the bottom of the fuel tank so, to drain it, we removed the sender, pumped out the tank, replaced the sender then taped a plug into the fuel tank breather to make sure nothing escaped.

1

UNDER SEAT STOWAGE

Stowage below the saloon seating was secured using the simple screw-and-string method we had used on the coolbox lid, but as it's hidden by cushions its inelegance didn't matter.

Picture hooks and mousing twine should keep saloon locker lids shut

CHART TABLE

Home to dividers, batteries, mobile phones, spectacles, and more, the chart table had to stay shut. We used a sliding bolt latch again. We should have placed netting across the bookshelf, too, and secured the locker beneath the navigator's feet.

A bolt keeps the chart table closed

CABIN SOLE

Although the sole was not screwed down, there were countersunk holes in each board, so clearly they had been secured at some stage. All we had to do was screw them down again. It's neither an elegant nor a particularly convenient way to secure the boards – fitting them with finger-operated latches would be much better. Another possible solution that emerged was to fit eyebolts beneath each board and run a line through them, secured in the engine bay perhaps. I'm sure you can think of others.

There wasn't enough space in the bilge to store anything but had there been, we would have secured netting, similar to that used in the galley and over the drinks locker. Perhaps one edge could be hemmed and a zip sewn on to it to make access easier. There was a fair amount of equipment stowed under the bunks so, like the sole, we screwed down the bunk boards to keep items in place. The finger-operated latch solution would work well here, too.

Sole boards are screwed down to keep them in situ

Secure roll: after modifications

On deck, we left the anchor secured in the bow roller, but tied a rope strop from toerail to toerail across the anchor locker to make sure the chain didn't break out. We also padlocked the cockpit lockers. Then the crane operator began the capsize, following the same method we had used in the unsecured 360° roll.

After the capsize, I stepped aboard and saw the anchor locker was still shut and the anchor secure in the bow roller. So far, so good. Entering through the forward hatch, the first thing I sensed, rather than saw, was that, in contrast to the chaos on the unsecured roll, this time there was general disorder in contrast to the chaos on the unsecured roll.

❝ Dick had been flung across the saloon table and was now lying face down... ❞

The amount of water shipped was quite surprising

All the cushions stacked themselves neatly to starboard

In the saloon I noticed that Dick, without his pilot berth lee strap, had been flung across the saloon table and was now lying face down on the cabin sole to starboard. Tom had broken a leg and was lying on the sole at the base of the companionway perusing a soggy Reed's Almanac. Unfortunately, he'd kicked the video camera above the chart table during the roll so we lost its recording of the second half of the first roll. The shattered remains of one or two plates, strewn over the chart table and starboard seating, confirmed that the crockery net hadn't been a complete success.

The sole boards were not awash but there was clearly a lot of water in the boat. The contents of the saloon seating lockers – the toolbag, flares and the file containing the ship's papers – were submerged. The chart table's bin lockers and shelves were brimful of water, too. Only one galley locker had opened, from which a plastic spoon escaped and wedged itself under a hand-hold. The saloon cushions had assembled themselves neatly in the starboard pilotberth. Apart from that, the Crash Test Boat seemed in fairly good shape after a 360° capsize.

Dick was thrown from the pilot berth on to the cabin sole. Apart from a broken plate, the saloon is very tidy.

What we learned

Even in these benign, controlled conditions, after two gentle 360° rolls, the chaos that reigned below was horrifying. It gave a harrowing glimpse of the terror that the crews must have felt in the early hours of Tuesday, 14 August, 1979, in the Western Approaches.

With repeated rolls and so many loose items in the saloon, life was no more than a game of Russian roulette. Indeed, of the 44 yachts that issued distress signals, over half did so because of 'concern for the general safety of the crew'. It's easy to be critical of those who abandoned boats that were later recovered afloat, but for someone who wasn't there, it's impossible even to imagine the living hell that their yachts had become.

In terms of what we learned, the state of the saloon after the unsecured roll confirmed that the simple, inexpensive measures we installed over the course of a couple of days, using the most basic tools had, almost without exception, worked perfectly.

Secured by a lee cloth, you would have nothing more threatening than a cushion to deal with. The amount of flooding would be extremely alarming but with bilges free of detritus you would be better able to deal with it.

Dick proved the value of lee straps and our changes have clearly made the saloon safer. The contrast is clear: a dishcloth and a broken plate were the only casualties of the secure role

All our dummies were damaged in the test

Sole boards, table leaves, charts, chargers, flares and cans littered the saloon. Complete disorder

How to avoid capsize

Tank tests reported in Peter Bruce's classic book, *Heavy Weather Sailing*, revealed that any yacht will capsize when hit beam-on by a wave taller than 55 per cent of the yacht's LOA. Today's lighter, beamier yachts are more prone to capsize and the figure is more like 40 per cent. Safety in extreme sea conditions has been compromised for speed and manoeuvrability, and comfort and space below. It's a compromise well worth the taking – provided you follow certain rules.

For years it's been the storm sailor's book of choice

Gather forecasts. In 1979, forecasting was an even more inexact science than it is today, so none of the competitors in the Fastnet Race would have had any idea what awaited them until it was unavoidable. Nor was the fitting of a VHF radio compulsory. A few with Long-Wave sets picked up broadcasts by Radio 4 and Meteo France but again, not until a few hours before the storm struck.

Today, forecasting has much greater accuracy and sources are abundant, on radio, online, via NavTex, GRIBs. 'I couldn't get a forecast' is no longer an excuse for finding yourself in challenging conditions. If you feel the conditions will take you outside your comfort or competency, stay alongside and spend the day doing something else

Never sail without at least one forecast

Right tools for the job. If you are planning to cruise higher latitudes, get the right boat. Forecasting and seasonal trends can help you avoid bad weather, you could be exposed on longer passages. Choose a boat with a STIX number greater than her LOA, a ballast ratio of 40 or above and a length/displacement ratio of at least 250.

If your sailing plans can't avoid storms, make sure your boat is up to the job, like this Swedish Malo 37

Storm tactics. Yachts are most vulnerable to capsize when beam-on to large waves, so a correctly deployed sea anchor will ensure your safety. In sailing terms, tactics employed during the 1998 Sydney-Hobart Race demonstrated that extreme seas are best taken head-on with your best helmsman. Running with storm jib or trysail, close reach across the troughs, head up into the crests then bear away sharply at the top to avoid slamming on the back of the wave.

Study storm tactics. Never get beam on to big seas as you're most likely to capsize

So how did we capsize a yacht?

Ready for testing in Ocean Village Marina

We had considered fitting a remote control autopilot and sending her across overfalls in a strong breeze with wind-over-tide, but not for long. The chance of losing her was too high and we wouldn't be able to conduct two controlled, identical rolls. We had to use a crane. Unfortunately, this also meant that at least half of the roll would be very sedate, nothing like the horror of the 1979 Fastnet Race. But the exercise still seemed valid in terms of the lessons we could learn.

WANTED: CAPSIZE EXPERT

Very few people know how to deliberately capsize a yacht – it's not a skill for which there's much call. But there was one among the friends of *Yachting Monthly* who did: solo round-the-world racing sailor Mike Golding. One of the safety checks required by IMOCA, the body that governs the Open 60s that race in the Vendée Globe and Barcelona World Race, is self-righting from an inverted position using the Open 60's canting keel.

To roll the Crash Test Boat, we needed attachments for the two massive crane strops and the solution, though flimsy-looking, received Mike's backing and held remarkably well. Using four shackles, 2x5m of 8mm Dyneema and two short lengths of Spectra, we made two lashings between the main and mizzen masts' chainplates to which the crane's

Mike Golding's advice was wise, reassuring and absolutely rock-solid

nylon lifting strops attached. Since we weren't actually lifting the boat, it was thought that this should be man enough for the job but, as with every other aspect of this test, nobody really knew what would happen.

Mike is a very busy man so we were hugely appreciative when he agreed to spend a morning with us looking at our plans, highlighting the defects and suggesting improvements. He was also there on the day to advise on improvements to the set-up and instruct the crane driver.

MDL PROVIDES THE LOCATION

MDL (Marina Developments Ltd) kindly agreed to make Ocean Village Marina, where Mike tests his yachts, available for the capsize, provided there was zero pollution. In our first meeting, Mike told us we would need to drain the engine oil and the diesel fuel tank, seal the dipstick and seal the crankcase breather. He also recommended that we check whether the engine had captive bolts. Without them, the it could leave its mountings and tear out the stern tube, or drop through the cockpit floor and into the marina. It would need to be secured in place. Although our batteries were strapped down, they were not sealed so we removed them to the pontoon where we could use them to run the bilge pump between rolls.

OSMOTECH UK GETS HER READY

Next we asked Mike Ingram, MD of Osmotech UK, based at Hamble Point Marina, to advise us on capsize preparations. He confirmed the engine mountings were definitely not to be relied upon and sent one of his crew to drill two holes in the engine bay's plywood and run a webbing ratchet strap across the top of the engine. He didn't like the look of the two-part washboards either. There was a large vent in one and they were considered too ill-fitting to fulfil their function. We didn't want to fill the boat with water and see her sink – the crane strop attachments we were using were not designed to lift her off the bottom – so Osmotech made a one-piece marine ply washboard fitted with a handle and two bolts to secure it in place.

Much of her gear was stripped out for the test to prevent pollution

A ratchet strap prevents the engine escaping

Battery straps contain these 'lethal missiles'

ABOVE DECK

Hamble rigger Alan Moore (pictured right) unstepped the masts because they would have broken during capsize. Originally, we had planned our dismasting test before the capsize test, but a lack of wind in spring 2011 and publishing deadlines meant we had to swap the tests. We also removed the granny bars and the lifelines, because the crane's lifting strops would have torn them out together with the stanchions. For the secure roll we added padlocks to the cockpit locker hasps, secured the anchor to the bow roller and secured a strop over the anchor locker to stop the chain spilling out. The strop was removed for the unsecured roll but the anchor remained tied. With no strop, we fully expected to be hauling 30m of chain off the bottom of Ocean Village Marina and we didn't want an anchor on the end of it. For both rolls, the lockers were emptied of everything that wouldn't float.

We unstepped the Crash Boat's masts at Hamble Pint

Though listing with a tonne of water in the starboard cockpit locker, the Crash Boat confirmed our test's success

READY TO GO

We set the date, prepared the boat, booked a crane and were ready to test on 7 April, 2011. I wanted to be onboard to experience the chaos first-hand, holed up in the relative safety of the forecabin. But the dangers were judged to be too great by risk assessment experts and insurers.

' Very few people know how to deliberately capsize a yacht – it's not a skill for which there's much call '

'Five minutes that changed my life'

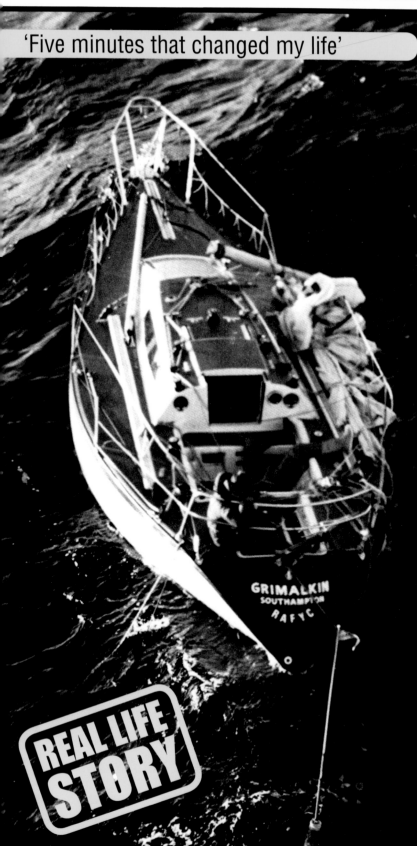

One of the most dramatic stories from the 1979 Fastnet Race involved the 30ft sloop, *Grimalkin*. Matthew Sheahan, a journalist on *Yachting World* magazine, recalls how the race ended in personal tragedy

I was 17 when it happened, and for the past 30 years the most frequently asked question has been: 'You must have been absolutely terrified. How on earth did you cope?'

For the first few years after the event I had no real answer. As anybody who has come close to death may tell you, your mind is paralysed. Being towed by your harness and accelerating down the face of waves behind a surfing boat under bare poles, you don't even know or care which way up you are. You have no idea what's going on. No time to panic. No time to shout. You are totally at the mercy of the elements.

During a long, terrifying night, *Grimalkin*, our Nicholson half-tonner, skippered by my father, had suffered numerous knockdowns and pitchpoles as we sailed across the Celtic Sea towards the Fastnet Rock.

Each crew member had frequently been towed along behind the boat by his harness after she had righted herself. The crew – my father David Sheahan, Gerry Winks, Mike Doyle, Nick Ward, Dave Wheeler – all had offshore racing experience.

***Grimalkin,** in which two crew died during the 1979 Fastnet. Photo credit: PPL Ltd*

REAL LIFE STORY

Matt Sheahean (right) with his father, David, on Grimalkin *before the capsize.* **Photo credit: Matt Sheahan**

But it was the last capsize that was the most frightening and the one that so easily could have cost six lives rather than the two as *Grimalkin* remained inverted for several minutes trapping all but myself under the boat. I remember thinking as I was pinned with my chin under the gunwale, held down by my life harness, this was the cruellest way to end it all. As the upturned hull lurched over the crests of the mountainous seas, I was momentarily released and had but a second to grab some air before the upturned deck bore down on my face again. As I struggled to get free, I was dragged under again, time after agonising time.

Because my harness only had a carbine hook at one end, and this was attached to a cockpit padeye, I could not free myself unless I took my harness off which meant taking my inflated lifejacket off first.

Although it was a struggle, I managed it and looped my right arm through the floating jacket as my left hand attempted to unfasten the harness attachment. Success! The buckle undid with the flick of a finger and, as the shoulder straps slackened, I floated a few centimetres higher, enough to let me breathe more freely.

And then, suddenly, everything changed. On this, our final knockdown, the mast had broken, and without its damping effect the boat righted in an instant. Suddenly, I could see part of the deck and was wrenched out of the water by my harness, fortunately still over my shoulders. I was launched across the full width of the cockpit.

Picking myself up off the windward deck, I looked around. I was no longer drowning but things were not looking good. Two people were unconscious (or possibly worse) in the cockpit. My father was floating face-down in the water and drifting away. Two conscious crew members were scrambling to get back on board.

' The last capsize was the most frightening. It was the one that could have cost six lives rather than two '

The word 'overwhelmed' seems too simple to express my reaction to the conditions. But what I've seen since 14 August, 1979, has frightened me more:

- Owners who pay scant regard to safety regulations or the serviceability of the safety equipment aboard their boats.
- So-called macho crews who deliberately avoid even sizing up a harness or lifejacket before a long offshore race, let alone wearing one when the going gets tough.
- Worst of all, those who believe it's unlikely to happen again.

When it comes to heavy weather survival, safety, in my book, is a state of mind. There is no definitive check-list of items and procedures, because safety afloat is a personal thing. It will depend on your experience, capabilities, type of boat and where you wish to sail. Safety is not yellow box with a set of batteries and a panic button. And it's certainly not relying on the Coastguard. Safety is thinking about the possible problems you might encounter and ensuring you've considered your options.

Dangers below deck are frequently ignored. One of the biggest problems aboard *Grimalkin* during the height of the 1979 storm was the ability of objects to break loose. Tins of food and other heavy objects were flying around the saloon each time we suffered a knockdown. I believe this was a factor which contributed to my father's death, despite everything being stowed in its correct place.

After the storm-damaged *Grimalkin* was recovered some weeks later, one of the lead acid batteries which had been secured under the companionway steps was found wedged in the yacht's bow. This deadly 'missile' had taken away part of the main bulkhead during one of our pitchpoles.

In the many articles and books written on the race, *Grimalkin* has been referred to as 'an orderly boat in a disorderly storm.' My father was a meticulous man who left nothing to chance. Everything was labelled, panic bags were clearly marked and every crew member briefed on the location of safety gear.

And yet, despite this organisation, in the space of less than 24 hours, I witnessed a competent boat and crew become overwhelmed by a series of events that ended in tragedy.

Perhaps the most important point is that our story is not about an instant crisis. We were not holed or run down. We did not lose our keel or rig (until the end) and there was no fire or explosion aboard the boat. Instead, we were faced with a series of events that escalated beyond our control. With the benefit of hindsight, I appreciate more than ever the importance of keeping your boat under control. Never let conditions overwhelm you. Safety is anticipating events both before and during your voyage. Safety begins well before you put on your lifejacket.

Daily Mail — WEDNESDAY, AUGUST 15, 1979 — 9p

MONEY MAIL

DISASTER AT SEA

30 lives feared lost ... 21 boats missing as a near hurricane hits yachtsmen

FASTNET RACE OF DEATH

By CHRISTOPHER WHITE and WILLIAM LANGLEY

A SEA disaster unparalleled in yachting history turned the Fastnet Race, the stern climax to Cowes Week, into awesome tragedy yesterday.

Braving the mountainous waves a Royal N man is lowered to a life-jacketed crew American yacht Ariadne in a desperate re

Turn to Page 2, Col 1

Sanyassa is towed backwards by two powerful RIBs hoping the stern would 'dig in' and she would do a backwards somersault and be righted. It didn't work. Photo credit: Vicky Bradley

Trapped inside a capsized boat

Clive Probert describes how his wife was trapped in an air pocket when their catamaran capsized in a freak mini-storm in Greece, in September 2011

Sanyassa, our Prout Snowgoose Elite, had been our home since 1997, when we left Pwllheli in North Wales to make a leisurely circumnavigation. One evening at 1800 we were anchored in a bay in Vlikho enjoying a gin and tonic down below when aware that our wind generator began making a screaming sound.

As I moved to the cockpit to start the engine the awning blew away like a paper napkin. My wife, Norma, start to emerge from down below as *Sanyassa* heeled to around 70° and water came over the cockpit seats. The next wave tilted us past 90° and the boat capsized. I was thrown into the water and surfaced alongside the upturned port hull. As I looked astern, I saw dimly through the torrential rain a monohull with its masthead in the water. I later learnt that this yacht had been knocked flat four times.

I was able to make my way aft and reach the upturned swimming ladder and climbed onto the inverted hull. Less than five minute ago I had been sitting in the saloon. The last thing I had seen as I was flung across the cockpit was Norma disappearing down below, sent there by the force of the water. I shouted her name and banged on the hull. At first I heard nothing, then I heard her shouting for help. She is a non-swimmer and I knew she would not be able to escape without help. How long would the air pocket she was trapped in last? By now other boats nearby had recovered and I shouted for help. Almost immediately, I saw Ruairi Bradley coming towards us at full speed in his RIB. He climbed onto the upturned hull gave me the painter and jumped into the water. He asked where the various hatches and main entrance was and disappeared behind the starboard hull. Another person then appeared in the water off the bow and asked where Ruairi was. I shouted to Norma and asked if Ruairi was with her. I heard her say 'Yes!' Within a minute there was a cheer and Norma and Ruairi appeared around the bow.

NORMA WRITES:

As the boat capsized I was thrown down the stairs into the port hull and swallowed a lot of water. I looked around my upside-down world and had difficulty recognising things. An environment one is so very familiar with looks so different the other way up. The water then started to come higher and higher inside the boat. I was very frightened and thought I was going to die... then the water stopped rising. It was up to my chest. I remember thinking: 'Well, at least the water is warm and I'm not going to die of hypothermia.'

Clive and I were managing to maintain some contact and he told me someone was coming to rescue me. I saw a dark shape below me and pulled it up into my air pocket. I know now it was Ruairi. He told me I would have to take a deep breath and swim out. And I don't even like water on my face in the shower! I tried to calm down and get some breath in my lungs and

not think about what I was about to do. I held tight to the back of the bib on Ruairi's oilskins. We swam out and I remember banging and crashing into things and then we were on the surface and I was being held in a life saving hold. I looked up and saw Clive standing on the hull. It was the best sight in the whole world. From capsize to rescue had been about 15 minutes.

Footnote: Four yachts in the area recorded winds around 100 knots. The most likely explanation for the freak wind that lasted for 10 minutes or so was thought to be a down-draught from a large thunderstorm cell. Waterspouts were also seen in the area.

Clive and Norma glad to be alive.
Photo credit: Rod Heikell

Total carnage is revealed as the Sanyassa is turned right side up at the quayside. Pictured aboard is Norma's rescuer Ruairi

3 DISMASTED

What happens and which tools work best?

The dismasting was controlled but the damage was real enough and the adrenalin was flowing

The mast: elegant, upstanding, unwavering – the very definition of seamanship under sail since the Egyptians first pioneered wind-powered trading vessels over 5,000 years ago. Without a mast, we are merely motorboaters. If it's free of structural defects, well maintained and you reef appropriately in strong winds, it will give years of sailing pleasure.

But what happens if it breaks? The best case scenario is an abrupt end to your day's sailing. You clear all lines from over the side and motor home with a slightly shaken but otherwise uninjured crew, and an expensive story to tell. The worst outcome is that the mast injures the crew, then its wreckage punctures the hull and your boat sinks.

To minimise the chances of a drama turning into a total disaster, it's vital to clear the wreckage and cut away the rigging quickly. But how effective are the £30 set of bolt croppers you bought from a DIY store several years ago? They will probably have been buried in a locker and be rusted solid by the corrosive marine environment. Can you use them on a wet, rolling deck when you need one hand for the ship? Will the jaws' scissor action cut through effectively?

These are some of the questions we wanted to answer. We researched every method we knew to cut shrouds so we could evaluate them in a real-life situation at sea. We ruled out a 12v angle grinder, which some recommend, because using electrical equipment on a wet, rolling deck is extremely hazardous.

Fuses break and the topmast falls off...

What happens when a mast breaks?

Paul Lees, from Crusader Sails, in Poole, Dorset, is a veteran of three dismastings. He forewarned the Crash Test Boat crew that a dismasting is actually fairly sedate process, because the sails slow down the action of gravity. Having experienced it for the first time, I'm not sure sedate is the word, but it certainly wasn't as violent as I had expected.

From my position at the genoa sheet winch, it looked at first as if the genoa halyard had parted but a split second later the mast collapsed with a crack that was just audible over the noise of the wind. The backstays settled across the cockpit, rather than scything down like cheesewires, as I had feared. Paul advised us that when the rig collapses, the safest places to be are down below, aft of the twin backstays or lying in the cockpit. We did as we were told and nobody was hurt. The most notable difference was the increased rolling.

Without the mast and sails to dampen the motion, the yacht rolled faster and more frequently. Moving safely on deck was a hands-and-knees affair, except for the youngest and nimblest crewman, Mark Lees. With the yacht's severe motion and a lack of lifelines, we all wore lifejackets – there was a very real risk of somebody falling overboard.

' The backstays settled across the cockpit rather than scything down like cheesewires ,

' To prevent a drama turning into a disaster, it's vital to clear the wreckage and cut away the rigging quickly ,

0.75 SEC   1.50 SEC   2.25 SEC   3.00 SEC

...still stayed by the lowers, the mast breaks...

...then the lowers' coquilles fall out...

...leaving the stump unstayed...

...and the whole lot goes over the side

We wanted to unfurl some genoa to break the fiberglass clevis pins, but accidentally it all rolled out. With the sail flogging, the mast had to break.

We didn't clip on with tethers for several reasons. We wanted freedom of movement in case several hundred kilograms of twisted aluminium suddenly decided to shift. Secondly, on a deck festooned with lines and shrouds, we would have been clipping and unclipping every couple of feet. Add to that the risk of accidentally clipping onto the lifelines, only to be dragged overboard as the mast slid over the side. It would be easy to get tangled in the wreckage and cordage and be dragged under.

RECOVERING THE WRECKAGE

The plan, which couldn't be completely formed until we knew what wreckage we were dealing with, was to secure the mast stump, then remove the boom gooseneck, the kicker and mainsheet and stow what we could below, including the mainsail, for potential jury rigging. This would also clear deck space. Next, the outboard end of the stump would be hauled alongside and inboard by securing lines around it and winching it within reach. With the stump secured, we would try to haul the top section alongside and repeat the process. This second stage promised to be far more difficult because of the weight of water in the genoa.

In the half-hour I spent testing the shroud cutting tools, the boom and mainsail were stowed below. The mainsail was freed by cutting the halyard – but the mast stump had slipped over the side. We spent nearly three hours hauling it back aboard, by which stage we had drifted five miles east, on wind and tide, to beyond West Lepe. We were too close to shipping lanes to continue our test, so we secured one end of a mooring line to the top section, tied a fender to the other and cut the forestay to ditch it (our support boat, Dave Kennett's motorboat, *Dunlin*, recovered it). After checking for lines over the side, we started the engine and motored home.

The lesson we learned about recovering a wrecked mast is that, on boats over 30–35ft, it's just not possible for an average coastal cruising couple. Saving the boom and mainsail was fairly easy and left us something to jury-rig. But getting the stump aboard was extremely hard work for four relatively fit and strong crew. The solution, if you're in shallow water, is to buoy the wreckage to enable recovery later, then cut it free. If you're in open ocean you'll have rather longer to recover the rig, but the sea state will make recovery even harder and the potential for holing far greater.

8–10mm wire rigging thrashes like baby snakes as the rig collapses. With the port-side cap shroud and D2 loose, it snapped at the weakest point, the lowers' coquille fittings, and tumbled over the side fairly gently, its descent slowed by the sails. Then the clear-up began

After securing the stump, the first job was to get the boom and mainsail below, clearing space on deck and leaving us enough kit for a jury rig. The main halyard was cut at the stump, the sail hauled down its track, the gooseneck unbolted and the lot moved below

While cutting away the rigging, the stump escaped the lashings securing it and slipped over the side. Rolling as we were, it could easily have punched through the hull. We managed to haul it back aboard, but it took four of us nearly three hours

Avoiding a hole in the hull

This is the big worry when a yacht is dismasted. We took some heavy gelcoat gouges in the topsides but the hull was not punctured. That may be due to the fact that our Francespar had hinged spreaders, riveted to the mast, that folded up as soon as the shrouds parted. Welded spreaders, or those supported through the mast by a rod, are stronger and would have offered the mast more support but they would also remain in place and present a greater danger of holing, making the need to ditch the spar all the more urgent.

DISMASTED AT NIGHT

Even during daylight, moving around the deck, cutting the right halyards and distinguishing lifelines from rigging wasn't as easy as you'd think. At night, I would have real concerns for the safety of anyone working on deck. A lifejacket, harness and lifeline are essential, as is a head torch. A decent multi-tool, in addition to your rigging cutters, is also recommended. Check the jackstays are secure before leaving the cockpit, as they may have been damaged during dismasting, and exercise extreme care on deck.

We had surprisingly little damage to the hull but it was obvious how easily we could have been holed

While we were cutting shrouds, the mast stump slipped over the side. We spent almost three hours hauling it back aboard and drifted five miles, close to the shipping lanes

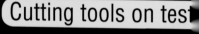

Cutting tools on test

After the mast fell to leeward, we took stock of the situation. The boat's momentum carried her round to windward of the rig, but with wind and waves pushing the hull downwind faster than the tide, the sails became a sea anchor, with the main doused to starboard and genoa ballooning to port. Within minutes, the yacht scraped back to leeward of the wreckage. Wind-rode, there she stayed, beam on to wind and waves, drifting east up the Solent's mainland shore.

Then we began to free the hull from the wreckage, pulling out clevis pins and cutting shrouds with various tools aboard. The Crash Test Boat had 8–10mm 1x19 stainless steel wire rigging. The deck was a hazardous zone: wet, covered with sails, rope and shrouds. Some of the starboard stanchions were torn out of the deck and the lifelines were down. Without her mast, the yacht was rolling like a fairground ride.

Nail pincers around £4   8/10

These came from photographer Lester McCarthy's expansive and well-maintained toolkit. He had several pairs, but I chose the ones with jaws that opened wide enough to grip the head of the clevis pin. If they don't, they're useless for this task. In our test, these performed better than the pliers, possibly because of their condition. The advantage of being able to clamp the jaws over the head of the clevis pin makes them better suited to the task than pliers. They can be used one-handed, too, but share the same problem as the pliers: no use if there is any load in the stay, or the bottlescrew's split pin is inaccessible.

Hacksaw with bi-metal blade around £23   9/10

It's a false economy to buy a cheap hacksaw, as I discovered. My £8.99 hacksaw, from a DIY store, had a plastic blade-retaining pin that soon snapped, so we used photographer Graham Snook's sturdy metal hacksaw with a stainless steel cutting blade – standard blades will blunt quickly when sawing through rigging. The leeward D2 shroud was heavily loaded and hanging over the rail. With the lifelines torn out and the boat rolling heavily, a two-handed tool would have presented real problems. I held the hacksaw with one hand and the mangled granny bars with the other. Though tricky to cut accurately, with boat and rigging moving independently, it took just 20 seconds to cut the shroud, strand by pinging strand.

It took just 20 seconds to cut through the shroud with a hacksaw

RigOff £116.20 each   7/10

Made by UK inventor Cameron Jemison, this is a bottlescrew that dismantles. A pair of two-piece rubber collars peel apart, two retaining flanges slide out and the centre section falls into three pieces. Production is small-scale, with Cameron looking for a licensee. If the product is successful, prices will come down. The RigOff was fitted to the heavily loaded leeward cap shroud. Despite lack of access to the underside,

removing the rubber collars was easy enough but the flanges didn't fall away and weren't going to be moved by hand. After a kick, the top flange fell away, followed by the second as the unit fell apart, as designed. It is one-handed, involves minimal effort and no tools but, under load, the flanges needed some persuasion. For information email cameron@rigoff.com

The RigOff is an ingenious bottlescrew that can be dismantled – with a kick!

Cable cutters around £160   4/10

These came from and Paul Lees's toolkit. Their primary advantage is that an indent in one blade holds the shroud captive. These are Swiss-made Felco cutters – a very decent pair, strong enough to cut six stays without damaging the blades – so they are expensive. Despite their size, bigger than the bolt croppers, the steel-cored aluminium handles made them much lighter, but they still required two hands. Without the mechanical advantage of the bolt croppers' cam action, they required far greater effort. With the stay held captive, I eventually placed one handle on the deck and leant all my weight on the other. They cut cleanly but there was no chance of using one hand for the ship.

The Swiss-made Felco cutters had an indent in one blade which held the shroud captive

Bolt croppers around £80   7/10

Again, we plundered Lester's tool kit and found two pairs of bolt croppers, one that opened just wide enough to enclose the rigging and another that could potentially have cut the mast in two. I chose the former. Made in Germany, the price and origin remain a mystery. I had expected the rigging wire to squeeze out of the jaws, requiring several chomps and damaging the blades, but they cut through at the first attempt. Using the proven technique of the full range of the handles and the built-in cam action, I needed less grunt than I expected. These were heavy, two-handed tools, so you need to brace yourself well. Good-quality bolt croppers are expensive.

Good quality bolt cropper are expensive. Brace yourself well as you cut

Hydraulic cutters (wire up to 14mm)

around £1,115   **7/10**

We borrowed these from Holmatro dealer The Rig Shop in Southampton. They arrived in their own dry bag and suffered no ill effects from their immersion during the capsize test. Due to the pressures involved, hydraulic equipment is generally heavily engineered and that's reflected in the price. They couldn't have been simpler to use: open the jaw and close it around the stay, then pump about 10 times. You can rest the handle on deck and operate it one-handed. They're simple, effective and involve minimal effort, but they're expensive and exclusively for cutting rigging. Visit www.holmatro.com for more information.

Holmatro's hydraulic cutters could not have been simpler to use, even one-handed

YACHTING MONTHLY RECOMMENDS

Pliers around £7   **7/10**

Every boat has a set of pliers. They're cheap to buy and easy to use one-handed. Ours were part of a budget Halfords toolkit. They were corroded after our capsize test but performed well in removing a split pin and drawing out the clevis pin on one of the twin backstays. It took a minute to free the backstay from its chainplate but, crucially, there was no load in the stay. Had there been, I couldn't have pulled out the clevis pin. It's also possible that during a dismasting a bottlescrew could fall so that the split pin was facing the deck, making it inaccessible without manhandling the shroud.

Pliers performed well in removing a split pin as well as a clevis pin from the backstay

Shootit around £499   **7/10**

Designed to cut through stays, this German-made device uses the same sort of explosive charge used in nail guns. Ours, borrowed from Safety Marine in Portsmouth, worked perfectly and involved much less drama than I'd imagined. Press the red button to open the chamber, slide in the charge strip, close it, cock it, hook the jaw around the stay, remove the safety catch and press the silver trigger. The

shroud was severed with absolutely no effort involved. It has no other uses, however, which affects its value-for-money score, and you can't board a plane with the explosive charges. Visit www.toolova.de for more information.

An explosive charge is used by the German-made Shootit to sever a shroud

What we learned

It may have been a test, but there was tension in the crew as well as the rig

YOU WILL NEED AT LEAST TWO RIG CUTTING TOOLS

The results were a surprise, but I stand by our findings, since I don't know of any other dismasted yacht crew that has tested every practical method of cutting shrouds in anger. Significantly, we proved that loaded and unloaded stays are very different beasts and it's a major advantage to have tools you can use one-handed, particularly when the lifelines have been swept away.

If you can afford them, the hydraulic cutters and the Shootit were the simplest, quickest and easiest ways to cut wire stays. A decent hacksaw, with bi-metal stainless steel-cutting blades, is also effective, can be used one-handed and has other uses. Make sure you have spare blades that are protected against corrosion.

Much to my surprise, the bolt croppers worked very well – much quicker and easier than the cable cutters, despite their weight and two-handed operation. But are you prepared to spend over £70 for a decent set that

Before the dismasting the split pin was accessible

you're unlikely to use? Probably not. A cheap pair, even if they haven't rusted solid, won't be up to the job of cutting six or more stays. If you choose bolt croppers, don't skimp, and make sure the jaws open wide enough to enclose the stay fully.

You will already have a pair of pliers or nail pinchers on board. For unloaded stays, they offer a simple, cost-effective, multi-purpose solution but they won't help on loaded stays. Don't even try. That amount of stainless steel whipping back at speed could cause serious injury.

The RigOff is a clever piece of engineering and a refreshing approach to the problem. Bearing in mind it was heavily loaded and the shroud was over the side, its slightly reluctant performance is still creditable. You would need at least six for an average sloop rig, so it's not cheap, but you'd save on the cost of six standard bottlescrews.

The forestay was the last to be cut, and the trickiest. With the furling gear surrounding the stay, removing the split and clevis pins was a good theoretical solution. However, during our dismasting, the toggle took such a battering, deforming as it fell across the anchor, that the split pin could not be removed. Even if it could, the forestay is almost certain to be loaded because of the genoa will turn into a sea anchor, so you will be unlikely to be able to remove the clevis pin.

With the forestay bent over the pulpit, the wire was exposed in one place, between the drum and the luff foil section. The gap wasn't wide enough to use the Shootit or the Holmatro cutters and it was moving around too much for hacksawing. Crusader Sails' Mark Lees clamped the cable cutters around the exposed wire and, after a few seconds contorting himself into a position where he could generate the required leverage, the stay parted.

After, the dismasting, the toggle was deformed

The hacksaw was cheap, and better on loaded stays than unloaded

There was no chance of removing the mangled split pin

How to avoid dismasting

1 CHECK YOUR RIG
Provided it's free of structural issues and barring a knockdown, a rig never just fails. There are always signs of imminent failure and they're not difficult to spot. Catch them in time and you will save your spar.

2 CHECK AND TAPE SPLIT PINS
They may seem insignificant but, make no mistake, a handful of properly fitted split pins will save your mast. Without them, bottlescrews and clevis pins work loose and you'll lose the lot. Use the biggest split pin that will fit the hole, pack any space with stainless steel washers, insert the pin, spread both its legs into an anchor shape and secure with tape or a blob of silicone.

3 CHECK SHROUD TERMINALS
Securing mooring lines to shroud bases is never a good idea because the loading can deform rigging toggles and weaken bottlescrews, creating uneven loading and increasing the chances of failure through fatigue. If there isn't a cleat handy, use genoa cars, winches or

padeyes, instead. For standing rigging, check the top of the swage and look for any broken strands. If you find some, replace that shroud and its opposite.

4 CHECK YOUR FURLER AND LINE
Check the furling line. Make sure the lead onto the drum is fair and that there are no chafe points. If it's looking tired, replace it. Remember, if the furling line breaks in a blow, you'll have far too much sail up for the conditions and the loads will be critical. Also, check the grub screws on the collar where the drum meets the luff tube. The forestay shakes tremendously during tacks and those grub screws can easily come loose. Secure them with PVC or Loctite.

5 SEND A RIGGER UP THE MAST
There is no tension in the stays of an unstepped mast, and that means broken strands can creep back into the swage, giving the appearance that nothing's wrong. Once a season, send a rigger aloft. He can check for broken strands at the top of shrouds, cracks in terminals, or in the mast around terminal fittings, and make sure your shackles are properly seized and your sheaves are in good order.

6 CHECK MAINSAIL TRACK SLIDERS, CARS OR BOLT ROPE
Just as a snapped furler line will leave you with far too much sail up, losing a few mainsail track sliders or tearing out your main's bolt rope can leave the sail bulging to leeward. In a matter of seconds the wind can strip out the others, leaving you with a spinnaker where your mainsail used to be. Check the fastenings to both mast and sail are secure and repair if you're in any doubt.

7 MANAGE YOUR CANVAS
The old adage states: 'If you're thinking about it, it's time to reef.' Barrelling along with the rail under is all good schoolboy stuff but it's neither comfortable nor especially quick and you are stressing the rig unnecessarily. You wouldn't drive your car at 50mph in second gear and a boat is no different.

8 TRIM SAILS PROPERLY
Leaving sails to flog – even that pesky bit at the top of the genoa's leech – shortens the life of the sail and shakes the entire rig. Get to know your sail controls and learn as much as you can about sail trim without laying yourself open to accusations of racing. Your sails and your rig will last longer and you'll enjoy sailing more – and cut a more experienced dash on the water.

How we did it

We needed at least 20 knots of wind for this test. We set out from Lymington Yacht Haven, in the Western Solent, with a forecast WSW Force 5–7, occasionally 8. Online weather reports from Bramblemet's website were recording a steady 30 knots. Despite wind-with-tide, we thought it would be more than enough.

We had an entire neap flood tide and a big stretch of water to play with before we would trouble any shipping. We made sure there was enough water to avoid digging the masthead into the seabed, 'pole-vaulting' the boat over the spar and risking damage below the waterline.

With three reefs in the mainsail and a third of the genoa unrolled, we were storming around at 9–10 knots. We planned to dismast her just above the first spreaders by replacing the clevis pins on the leeward cap shroud and D2 with short lengths of 10mm fibreglass batten, or 'fuses', while on starboard tack, then tack over, harden up and wait for the bang. Mark Lees and Jerry Henwood went forward to insert the 'fuses', taped them up and came aft. The battens were far stronger than anyone thought – the rig didn't budge. 'Next time someone tells me they've broken a batten, I'm going to ask them how they did it!' marvelled Paul.

Undeterred, we wore around, gybing heavily enough to pull a mainsheet block off the boom. We replaced the 10mm battens with 6mm, tacked onto port again and waited. And waited. Finally, Paul called for more headsail and Mark accidentally let it all out. With the genoa shaking violently, the loads were finally high enough for the battens to shear.

Unstayed, the top of the mast arched to leeward. With a full genoa on a sagging forestay in 30 knots of wind, and the lowers holding the first spreaders in place, the mast took on an S shape as the extra compression loading crushed it on its step. Three seconds later the masthead hit the water.

The break was at the point where the coquille terminals for the fore and aft lowers were positioned. These require four apertures in the mast and, once the cap shroud and D2 had parted, that was the weakest point. The coquilles for the lowers then sprang out, leaving the stump unsupported. It bounced off its step and fell overboard.

> ‘ We set out with a WSW Force 5–7, occasionally 8. Bramblemet was recording a steady 30 knots ’

We lost the genoa but the only damage to the main was the tear at its luff

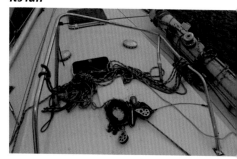

The mast crushed the granny bars and took out the lifelines on its way over the side

The Crash Test Boat had a thick mast section and it took a lot of breaking, reassuring for all

The egg-shaped holes for the lower coquilles proved to be a weak point. That's where it broke

Sea dark, sky crying

Clockwise from top left: Isabelle is reunited with her shore crew Serge Viviand. Wearing her survival suit and talking by VHF radio to rescue planes. The shattered cabin roof

Isabelle Autissier, the only woman competing in the 1994–95 BOC Challenge Round the World Singlehanded Race, was forced to abandon her crippled yacht deep in the Southern Ocean, plucked by helicopter at the limits of rescue services.

It took just a split second and an unavoidable slam on the portside for Isabelle Autissier's dreams to suddenly come toppling down around her. A rigging screw on her yacht's main port shroud failed and the mast collapsed over the starboard side, snapped at the base.

It was December 2 and the 38-year-old French yachtswoman, a marine science professor and engineer, was halfway between Cape Town and the Kerguelen Islands on the seventh day of the second leg of BOC Challenge Round the World Singlehanded Yacht Race.

Her 60ft rocket ship *EPC2* had streaked away down the Atlantic from the September start in Charleston, South Carolina, America, to win a decisive victory in the first leg of the race, leaving the men, her fellow competitors,

1,200 miles astern battling in her wake for second place.

Now she was the southernmost boat in the fleet of 14, reduced from 18 that began the epic race. 'I felt like I had been hit in the stomach. I thought "No. Not this. Not here." It was already over for me. But what was the use of yelling, shouting and crying for a victory that was completely lost?' Isabelle recalled. She sent a message to Race HQ in Charleston: 'Dismasted. No danger immediately.' She was 1,200 miles from Cape Town, and lying at 48 degrees 52m south.

There was no time to waste. A mast can become a horrific hammer of carbon fibre threatening to puncture the hull of a yacht. The winch at the foot of the mast was already starting to smash a hole in the deck. With a hacksaw, pliers and a knife, Isabelle scrabbled about on her knees cutting away the rig as the yacht rolled. The water temperature was just three degrees and water was flying everywhere. She tried to save the boom, but it broke, dragged down by the weight of the mainsail. Ninety minutes later, she had cut away most of the rig and stood on the bare deck of her yacht. She had one complete spinnaker pole and half of a broken one. 'There are 5,000 miles left to Sydney. I feel so much like crying for my lost hopes. But this is the way racing goes.' By evening she had managed to put the small pole at the mast foot, ready to use it as a support for raising the main nine-metre pole as her replacement mast the next day.

She had suffered a dismasting four years ago on this same leg of the BOC Challenge, south of Tasmania. On that occasion, the mast broke at the first spreader and she fashioned a jury rig and sailed into Sydney Harbour to step a new mast. Once again the only woman in the race, she gained many admirers by going on to complete her circumnavigation.

At the crack of dawn the next day, Isabelle began work afresh on erecting an emergency mast. Using her small five-metre broken spinnaker pole, with a halyard rigged from the top, she raised the nine-metre pole. 'It sounds easy, but in the bad weather it took me 24 hours crawling on my hands and knees,' she said.

'I'll forget about the second leg. My goal is to arrive in Sydney with enough time to make preparations to start leg three with the others.' Under two tiny headsails, Isabelle set course for Kerguelen Island, a remote French outpost some 1,200 miles away that was home to weather and scientific research stations. Two days later, when the sun was out, she worked to reinforce the base of her new mast with epoxy glue and carbon fibre. She wound a length of small diameter rope around the mast and glued it together to add thickness at the foot. In the damp conditions, to help it dry, she made a tent around the mast and used her small emergency generator inside to add warmth. *EPC2* was averaging four knots and was expected to arrive at Kerguelen Island in 13 days.

Sources in France confirmed that a replacement mast for her yacht had been found on Reunion Island and was being shipped to Kerguelen on a French cargo vessel. Two weeks later, sailing under jury rig, Isabelle – dubbed `Isabelle the Incredible' – arrived at Kerguelen Island, eager to re-rig her yacht with the replacement mast which had, meantime, arrived on a supply ship from Reunion Island. A cargo boat carrying sails and equipment was due to arrive the following night. It was snowing hard and the winds were over 40 knots as *EPC2* was towed into the protected harbour by a French scientific vessel conducting studies in the Antarctic region.

After a three day stop at Kerguelen, Isabelle had converted *EPC2* from a single-masted sloop into a double-masted yawl, using her spinnaker pole as a mizzen mast. Her new 13m main mast was from a much smaller Figaro Solo yacht and a set of sails had been donated by French yachtsmen.

But 12 days later on 28 December, the 32nd day of leg two, disaster struck again. Nearly 1,000 miles southeast of Adelaide, Isabelle was sailing under bare poles in winds howling at 60-70 knots. 'It was then that I heard it coming . . . like a powerful locomotive. I instinctively crouched down. I knew it was going to flatten the boat.' A monster wave crashed over the yacht, launching it through a semi-pitchpole, end-over-end, tearing the away the masts like matchsticks. At the same time the yacht did a corkscrew through 360°. Isabelle was thrown onto the roof, choked by a rush of ice-cold water. 'I could feel it rolling. I fell on the bulkhead, then on the ceiling, then on the other bulkhead. If I had been on deck I would have been washed away.'

The whole incident lasted less than 20 seconds. Isabelle stared in disbelief at a gaping hole of five square metres where the coachroof had exploded under water pressure. Over the next three days, huddled in a survival suit, she waited anxiously for rescue which came on New Years Eve, thanks to the Australian Navy and Air Force.

Extract from* The Loneliest Race, *by Paul Gelder (Adlard Coles Nautical).

REAL LIFE STORY

A 36ft Westerly Corsair, similar to Barbary Duck, sailing in the Solent. Photo Credit: Colin K. Work (www.pixstel.com)

Improvise or abandon ship?

The ability to improvise at sea when things go wrong is considered to be a mark of good seamanship. Famous French solo sailor Yves Parlier (pictured left) is nicknamed 'The extra-terrestrial' for his amazing exploits and capabilities. He once built a new carbon fibre jury rig after being dismasted during the 2000 non-stop Vendee Globe Round the World Race. He created an 'oven' from survival blankets heated by 25-watt light bulbs, candles and gas. But such resourcefulness is rare among ordinary mortals. Sometimes things go terribly wrong and yachts which could be fixed are abandoned.

John Weller, from Northern Ireland, and his wife Frances, left La Gomera in the Canaries, on 22 November, 2007, bound for Martinique in their Westerly Corsair, *Barbary Duck*. Six days out their engine failed. They discovered it was flooded and the water trap was full. They decided to divert to the Cape Verde islands, about 250 miles south-east. When they found their 36ft yacht was only making two knots, they changed course to the Caribbean. On Day 7 John suffered a serious head injury when the spinnaker pole came off the mast mounting. His wife, a nurse, used paper stitches to staunch the wound.

On Day 10 in squalls the toggle part of the rigging screw on the lower starboard shroud parted and was being held in place only by the clevis pin. Fearing they were in danger of dismasting, John put out a Pan Pan and yacht *GiGi*, a Swan 48, taking part in the Atlantic Rally for Cruisers, responded.

John tried a makeshift repair on the shroud with a sail tie but it failed so the couple dropped all sail. 'We felt very reluctant to go forward. Either one of us could have been killed by a boom, pole or mast falling on us,' John said later. He then broadcast a Mayday and *GiGi* again responded. Before taking to their liferaft, the couple switched on the masthead tricolour and set the Aries windvane self-steering, leaving the boat making a course of 270 degrees. They were rescued from their liferaft, some 600 miles north-west of the Cape Verde islands, by *GiGi*, and continued across the Atlantic to Rodney Bay, St Lucia.

Some weeks later a fisherman spotted *Barbary Duck* sailing herself off the island of Antigua. He towed her in and registered a salvage claim with the boat's insurers. Some of her equipment had been looted and the top section of her mast had broken. But her skipper, John, was 'delighted' she had sailed herself to the Caribbean. He flew out to meet an insurance surveyor to assess the damage.

Some commentators unkindly referred to the incident as 'a bad case of premature evacuation' adding that 'the usual advice is only step up into the liferaft when the boat is sinking beneath you.' This case followed two other yachts abandoned but not scuttled during the 2006 ARC, and later washed up – one in the Caribbean and the other in the Azores. An insurance expert said: 'There are important lessons from this case and others where yachts have been abandoned, which should be drummed into people before they set off. The most important was learned during the 1979 Fastnet Race – that the safest place to be, until the water is coming up around your neck, is the yacht herself. Nearly every year there will be a case like this where a yacht is abandoned and which subsequently turns up 8–12 weeks later in the Caribbean, which is where her crew were headed in the first place.'

The consensus among many is that if you can't jury rig a yacht you should sink her if you abandon her to avoid a danger to others.

Geoff Pack, former editor of *Yachting Monthly*, referring no doubt to the modern compensation culture, set against the seaman's watchwords of self-help, self-sufficiency and self-reliance, once said: 'Being uninsured is the best teacher of good seamanship and may, paradoxically, prove to be an advantage.' In other words the sailor who cannot climb into his liferaft with the certainty he can collect the insurance money may be more focused on having the equipment and skills to try and save his sinking or crippled boat.

Stepping into the liferaft, who could have imagined their abandoned yacht would sail herself across the ocean to the Caribbean? Photo Credit: Shin Terasawa

4 JURY RIG

How to make a jury rig that will get you home

If you're 'lucky' enough to be dismasted within motoring range of a port, all you need to do is cut away the rig, buoy the wreckage and note its position, assuming the water is shallow enough to recover it, then clear lines from over the side and start the engine. However, if you're outside motoring range, you'll need to be a bit more self-sufficient.

Unless you have a seriously injured crew member, or the hull has been holed, you are not in 'grave and imminent danger' so you may struggle to justify pressing the button to activate the EPIRB (Emergency Position Indicating Radio Beacon), if you have one. Also bear in mind that, without your masthead-mounted VHF radio antenna, your hand-held VHF range is limited to maybe 10 miles, so calling for assistance could be tricky, too. You could start firing distress flares but, unless there are boats around you, there is very little evidence to suggest you are not wasting your time, as well as your flares.

However, you can take charge of your destiny by using the wreckage salvaged after your dismasting to set up a jury rig and get yourself home. The stump of our mast was the biggest piece of wreckage we'd salvaged, so we opted to use that – the bigger the rig, the more sail you can carry and the quicker you'll get back. Re-stepping a mast stump is the most challenging procedure in jury rigging, because of its weight.

The yacht's genoa acted like a sea anchor, and making the forestay difficult to cut away

' The bigger the rig, the more sail you can carry and the quicker you'll get back '

Making a jury rig and testing it

With a brisk Force 4 southwesterly waiting to test our results, we set to work. Once again, Crusader Sails' Paul Lees was our consultant – he has been dismasted three times and managed to sail home under jury rig on each occasion. Our best chance of maximising sail area was to restep our 5m (16ft 5in) stump, use the main boom as a yard and cut the mainsail to make a squaresail.

The first task was to assess exactly what equipment we had to work with. We needed lots of line, plenty of stout blocks, some 8–10mm shackles and sails, so we emptied our lockers, stripped blocks from the boom, lines from the stump and assembled all our kit in the cockpit.

The plan was to create a tripod of stays. We ran a forestay from the masthead through a block at the stemhead – the strongest one we had available, because this stay would carry the greatest load – and back to a halyard winch. The two shrouds were run from the masthead through two blocks lashed to toerails aft of the mast step and back to primary winches. The halyard winch was large enough to get sufficient load on the forestay and the primaries had the fairest lead from the toerails. An auxiliary backstay was also rigged, but wouldn't be needed for the stepping.

It's not rocket science. Work out what you have and how you can use it

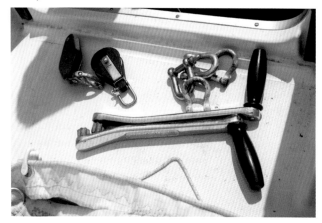

Our first task was to assess exactly what equipment we had to work with

Shroud base blocks were lashed through the block, not the swivel

With so much torn aluminium at the masthead, I wondered how we would attach stays with any hope of them not chafing through, but I needn't have worried. Paul had an ingenious solution. He pulled the pin out of a 10mm shackle and fastened an 8mm shackle through one half of it. The 10mm shackle was then hooked over the stump's masthead, leaving a nice smooth 8mm shackle to which rigging could be connected. This was repeated four times for the four stays and the shackles were duct-taped into place.

The shrouds were then attached using bowlines and run through their respective blocks. Also, remember to rig the halyards – one fore and one aft – before stepping the mast. We attached turning blocks to our shackle shroud terminals. For shrouds, we had to use standard 10–12mm multibraid rope, formerly used as sheets and halyards, in the knowledge that there would be a fair amount of stretch under the loads needed to hold the stump in place. Dyneema would have been a better choice – every boat should have some – but we only had a couple of 1m lengths and they were used to lash the shroud blocks to the toerails. We rigged the Dyneema through the blocks – between the cheeks and below the sheave – rather than through the blocks' swivels, because the swivel is the weak point of a block.

1. Interlinked 8 and 10mm shackles were used to create ingenious rigging terminals at the top of the stump's masthead

2. The linked shackles then hook over the jagged stump, creating rigging terminals

3. The backstay terminal is knocked into place next to forestay and shrouds

4. Four sets of linked shackles are taped into place at the new masthead

Next, using turning blocks at the foot of the mast and blocks at the step, we rigged a line that could be tightened to keep the mast's foot on the step during the stepping, preventing it from sliding off onto the sidedeck and over the side. Don't be tempted to guide the mast foot by hand. The boat will be rolling heavily and if the mast foot slips, it could injure you or damage the boat.

We rigged a line that could be tightened to keep the mast stump's foot on the step

Now it was time to raise our stump. We were fortunate to have a standby vessel, a RIB from SeaStart, the marine breakdown service, to keep us head-to-wind. Otherwise, we would have considered dragging the anchor or deploying some sort of drogue, a bucket for instance, off the bow to avoid lying beam-on to the sea. The mast's head and foot were under control but we certainly felt safer working with the boat's rolling minimised. Paul and I shouldered the stump as far as we could, taking a few moments to make sure the mast foot was on its step and not the coachroof. Then in the cockpit, Andrew winched in the forestay while Mark eased the shrouds

1. Paul shoulders the stump into place while the shrouds are eased
2. At this stage it's important to make sure the mast is still on its step
3. Andrew winches the forestay taut as Mark gently eases the shrouds

❛ If the mast foot slips as the boat rolls it could injure you or damage the boat ❜

Paul cuts the main just above the third reef to create the squaresail that will get us home

The boom would be our square rig's yard arm, with the second and third reefing lines as braces

With the foot of the re-cut main fastened to the boom we hoisted our sails

evenly to keep the masthead on the centreline. Once in place, with its foot on the step, the forestay and shrouds were winched in hard to take up the stretch and keep the foot in position. They were then secured to prevent accidental release.

CUTTING NEW SAILS

Having re-stepped the mast, the next job was to look at the sail area. The mainsail was the biggest and most useful sail, though we also had a short-luffed jib, similar to a storm jib, and an old cruising chute. We created our squaresail by cutting the mainsail about 30cm (1ft) above the third reef, which included much of the third reef's reinforcement.

We had planned to cut above the second reef. As it happened, three reefs was perfect, but it's worth checking twice before cutting. We planned to rig the sail upside-down by lashing the foot to the boom and using the third reefing points as clews, so the reef's reinforcement would prevent the reefing, now clew cringles tearing out of the sail.

We identified the second and third reefing lines in the boom, tied stopper knots in one end of one and the other end of the other, and pulled them through up to the knot. These would be braces for our yard, so that we could orientate it from the cockpit. In fact, the

braces weren't long enough to reach the pushpit base turning blocks and needed extending with other lines. The knots joining them jammed in the turning blocks so it might have worked more smoothly had we connected longer braces directly to the yard rather than using the reefing lines.

We used one of the mast's winches to haul the yard up to the masthead on our fore halyard

Next, the squaresail was lashed to the boom upside-down using the tack and clew. We attached sheets to the third reef's leech and luff cringles and ran them back to the secondary winches through the genoa sheets cars, and tied on a couple of sail ties to control the sail. After attaching the fore halyard to a loop of Dyneema lashed to the middle of the yard, we untied the sail ties and hoisted our square rig. Downwind, the rig worked well and we clocked up 2.5 knots easily. It took a few minutes to adjust to using braces and sheets but we soon got the hang of it and gybed – or more accurately 'wore ship' – through 160° true a couple of times before trying to

" We created a squaresail by cutting the mainsail about 30cm above the third reef "

bring her upwind. At 3–4 knots, we struggled to get above a beam reach. We needed to barberhaul the sail to get more luff tension, so we attached lines to the clews and ran them through forward cleats, then back to the cockpit. This improved our pointing but we still couldn't get her above 70° to the apparent wind on either tack, and speed slowed to 2.5 knots.

In an effort to improve windward performance we dropped the squaresail and hoisted the small jib as a trysail with the tack as head, clew as tack and head as clew. We pointed better with the trysail, but the drastic reduction in sail area slowed us and we made a lot of leeway, so effectively our progress to windward worsened. Then we rehoisted the squaresail and braced it as close as we could. Pointing improved 10° to around 60° apparent, but speed was still only 2.5–3 knots. Initially, we ran the trysail's sheet through the pushpit base, but the squaresail was backwinding the trysail so we moved it to the binnacle.

1. Our square rig works! There are lots of chafe points and obvious improvements but the concept is sound

2. The sheets and braces took a little while to get used to but soon we were gybing and tuning for better speed

3. Barberhaulers rigged through forward cleats helped us to generate more luff tension

4. To increase sail area, we hoisted the square sail. Speed improved, we made less leeway and pointed better

What we learned

Raising a jury rig is a challenge, just when you could do without one, but it's far from impossible. The ability to cope with any disaster scenario – assess the problems and figure out a solution – increases your self-sufficiency as a yachtsman and helps make you a better sailor. That's what the Crash Test Boat project is all about.

Having saved whatever you can after dismasting, take stock of the situation. Gather all your blocks, shackles and lines and plan your rig. Think about which winches do which jobs. If there aren't enough turning blocks, what else could you use? Cleats, padeyes and pushpit bases should work. Pool your resources and make a plan.

HANG IT HIGH
With the shrouds and forestay occupying three winches, we had to run two braces, two sheets and two barberhaulers on three winches with two crew

Our jib, now a trysail, helped pointing but didn't generate enough power on its own

so we ended up using trucker's hitches and cleats on some of the running rigging and prioritising procedures before manoeuvres.

Regardless of how clever your jury rig is, you're never going to match the sail area you had before dismasting. The key to a successful jury rig is sail area – the more you have and the higher up it is, the better it will perform. That's why we chose to raise the stump, the longest piece of wreckage onboard. If we had thousands of miles to go, we could have lashed the boom to the stump to make a taller rig and used the spinnaker pole as a yard for a square rig, or rigged fore-and-aft, maybe using the spinnaker pole as a mizzen. The possibilities are limited only by your kit and your imagination.

STEPPING THE MAST
It took about a minute to get the stump from horizontal to vertical. It was lighter than I'd expected,

First we stripped any useful lines from the mast stump. We needed all the line we could get

Our chainplates were blocks lashed to the toerail with Dyneema

and fairly easily handled by two people, even on a rolling deck, thanks to the line holding the mast foot in place and the shrouds keeping the masthead midships. Had it been too heavy to raise off the deck, we would have needed to fashion a gin-pole, possibly using the spinnaker pole on one of the mast step padeyes with lateral bobstays to both toerails. The forestay could then be run down to the stem and back to a winch via a hitch at the outer end of the pole, then winched vertical. Once your rig is in place, there'll be a noticeable reduction in the speed and frequency of rolling. Even our small stump dampened movement and the boat was a more comfortable place for it.

WHICH WAY IS SAFETY?

As we've established, if the nearest safe refuge lies to windward, a fore-and-aft rig is really your only choice. To get the height required to make it work, you will need to lash two bits of wreckage together. In a previous jury rig test (*Yachting Monthly*, January 2006), the boom and spinnaker pole were lashed together and storm sails hoisted. The team also used trucker's hitches on jury shrouds secured to midships cleats to get the required tension, which frees up the winches.

FORE-AND-AFT JURY RIG

In 2006, the *YM* team achieved 3 knots to windward

and a tacking angle of 100° in 15 knots of true wind. The test made no mention of leeway, but it did state that, in 20 knots, the lashing was 'over-stressed.' It's also worth noting that the 2006 jury rig was created and stepped in port. The lashing between the boom and spinnaker pole is the key to this rig and at sea, creating something secure enough to take on headwinds could be challenging.

RIG OPTIONS

It's quicker and easier to hoist sails in a fore-and-aft configuration but, with our shorter stump, so little of the sail area was up in the stronger winds a few metres above sea level that it generated much less power. The result was more leeway than headway, thus defeating the object. We did consider using the jib on the forestay, but having developed disappointing power as a trysail, it would have been next to useless with most of its area so close to the deck.

We also considered heading downwind with the cruising chute flying upside-down from the yard and appropriately 'wine-glassed' with a sail tie, but its asymmetric shape would have created a lop-sided rig and it would need hoisting outside the forestay. Though you have a finite number of sails, you have endless choice about how to fly them to get the most sail area at the greatest height. We opted for a squaresail rig. We could have clawed our way off a lee shore gradually but, as square-riggers have proved for centuries, we weren't going to sail well to windward. We had a decent rig for half the compass.

RIG TUNING

If we were expecting to take a few days to get home, we would have plenty of time to play around with the rig and sails, refining both, to iron out the problems and eke out the extra tenths of a knot in the directions we could sail. I saw lots of chafe points, the mast turned slightly on its foot and the windward shroud's stretching canted the mast – so much so that we secured the fore halyard's tail to the windward toerail to act as a second shroud.

> **' If the nearest safe refuge lies to windward, a fore-and-aft rig is really your only choice. '**

In 2006, YM's team lashed a boom and spinnaker pole together, hoisted storm sails and made 3 knots to windward with their fore-and-aft rig

How we set up the test

‛ Apart from a bag of shackles, we used nothing that wasn't on the boat already ,

PICK A WINDY DAY

Due to the rigours of her life, the Crash Test Boat engine's starter motor had packed up, so we asked SeaStart's Nick Eales to tow us with his RIB from Hamble Point Marina into the Solent, just south of Hillhead, and stand by. To stop us drifting onto Hillhead's lee shore, Nick held us in position while we prepared our rig – in open water this wouldn't have been a problem. Once ready to hoist sail, we dropped the tow.

With so little sail area, we needed at least a Force 3 to get the boat moving. On the day we had a decent Force 4, gusting 5. Apart from a bag of shackles, we used nothing that wasn't on the boat already. The mast stump's height and strength were important in its selection for the jury rig but also, having spent over two hours recovering it, following our dismasting, we were understandably keen to use it.

Epic voyage under jury rig

Dismasted yachtsmen have recorded many long-distance passages under jury rig. British sailor Robin Davie won the Ocean Cruising Club's Award of Merit for his epic 2,700-mile stint under jury rig around Cape Horn in his 40ft Hurley Tailwind, *Cornwall*, in the 1994–95 BOC Challenge solo Round The World Race.

Davie was dismasted at night in a 30-knot squall while running downwind in the Southern Ocean, 2,100 miles from Cape Horn. As the yacht rounded up, the poled-out headsail backwinded. Woken by the bang, and the boat shaking, he was out of his bunk and stepping into his oilskins and boots, fireman fashion, as *Cornwall* lurched drunkenly.

The mast had broken 7ft above deck. 'It was a surreal scene as the masthead light beamed brightly at a strange sideways angle, illuminating the sheared mast and torn sails in a swirling snow squall. I didn't know whether to laugh, cry, feel afraid or just plain cheesed off,' said Davie. A quick crawl around revealed little chance of salvaging much. It took 40 minutes to cut away the wreckage before it damaged the hull or deck, using hacksaw and wire cutters.

At daybreak, Davie fashioned a jury rig using his two spinnaker poles as an A-frame, set up 20ft from the bow. He cut up some aluminium sheeting to put under the feet and prevent damage to the deck, and taped the radio antenna up the length of the backstay so he could restore radio communications. Over the next few days he strengthened the jury rig with extra ropes, stays and guys. 'I knew that storm-force, even hurricane-force winds and big seas would find me and I didn't want to lose the rig in a knockdown,' he said.

The second day after dismasting, the resourceful solo sailor hanked on the upside-down staysail from the bow. In 20 knots of wind, *Cornwall* surged forward, albeit at only 3 knots. When the wind piped up to 30 knots, the boat speed increased to 4.5 knots. The

Davie's A-frame, made from two spinnaker poles. Photo: Kate Ford

rig seemed strong, so he set a storm jib behind the A-frame as a trysail. In the first few days, his 24-hour run rose from 62 miles to 92 on the third day and 125 miles on day five. In the first storm, *Cornwall* sped along at 6 knots. Beyond 40 knots, it was time to take down the storm jib. 'Under bare poles we were doing 6.5 knots in breaking seas!' he said. 'Speed was my safety. Slowing up in the storms was dangerous.' In two days of big winds, he covered 300 miles. It took Robin 24 days to reach Port Stanley in The Falklands, where a new mast had been shipped out.

'A dismasting is one of those things that could happen to any of us,' he said. 'It tends to ruin your day at the time, it was an experience I'll never forget and would never wish on anybody, but on the other hand I wouldn't have missed it for the world. So, take two spinnaker poles with you whenever you go offshore!'

Extract from **The Loneliest Race,** *by Paul Gelder (Adlard Coles)*

Could you make a jury rig?

Derek Bunting and his wife Anthea were faced with abandoning ship in mid-ocean when they were dismasted. They had nothing left to make a jury rig and suffered engine failure.

Sailing *Sukanuk*, their Tradewind 33, the Buntings left the Canary Islands on 5 December, 1999, with the 20-month Blue Water Round the World Rally. Nine days later, the starter motor failed and the emergency starting handle and decompression levers on their Yanmar 3GM30 engine also failed.

On Christmas Eve, 560 miles from Antigua, grey clouds started to build astern. They had already encountered Atlantic squalls but within an hour they faced their most violent squall as winds suddenly increased to 40–45 knots in the darkness. Anthea took the tiller as Derek released the starboard sheet to spill some wind. There was a cracking noise and a whoosh as the mast crashed over the port side.

Derek tried to salvage as much of the rig as possible, wearing a head torch to leave his hands free. The deck-stepped mast had torn away from its casting, leaving seven feet standing. The rest was crumpled on the port side toe rail and dangled 90 degrees down into the ocean having smashed the guard-rails and two stanchions. To prevent more damage he cut all the rigging free.

They lost the mast, boom, two spinnaker poles, a fully battened mainsail, furling genoa, working jib and furling gear and rigging. Apart from the working jib and furling gear, all were brand new and had only been fitted five months ago.

As they were now a danger to shipping, they broadcast a Satcom message, having jury-rigged an aerial, to Falmouth Marine Rescue Co-ordination Centre, and received a message that a ship, M/V *Benguela Stream*, had altered course to assist them. All the Buntings needed was help to re-start their engine, as they had more than enough fuel to motor

to Antigua. But the captain of *Benguela Stream* was only prepared to take them on board to South America, which would have meant abandoning *Sukanuk*. Several yachts in the area, including *Discovery II*, a 40-footer just 30 miles away, offered items, including an old spinnaker pole, to make a jury rig. But weather conditions intervened. *Discovery* tried towing them, but the tow kept breaking. Finally, on Boxing Day a message came from fellow Blue Water Rally yacht, *Tigre*, a 54ft Nordia Van Dam, which had already arrived in Antigua. Owned by Peter and Tania Hopkinson, she was designed for ocean cruising and could tow 200 tons with her Perkins six-cylinder diesel engine.

Rally yachts loaned the Hopkinsons 55 cans containing 1,400 litres of diesel which were strapped to the decks. They also carried an array of spinnaker poles, ropes and sails to make a jury rig, although towing always seemed the most likely solution. Their 1,000-mile round-trip mercy mission was the equivalent of sailing from Torquay across Biscay, and taking a yacht in tow off NW Spain to bring it all the way home! *Sukanuk* eventually arrived safely in Antigua on New Year's Day 2000. The moral of the story is: on a long offshore passage you must salvage as much as you can to make a jury rig – and carry back-up spare rigging, too.

5 SINKING

How do you stop a boat sinking?

The chances of being holed below the waterline in a collision are remote, whether you hit rocks, a floating log, or a shipping container. But as they say, accidents happen and worse things happen at sea, so we decided to put to the test various methods to stop a boat from sinking.

The chances are you'll know about a collision the second it happens. Once you've recovered from the shock, you will need to heave-to, as the damage is likely to be on the leeward side. Assuming there are two of you aboard, get your crew to prepare the grab bag and liferaft and then start using the manual bilge pump in the cockpit. If it's not already working, switch on the automatic bilge pump and send out a DSC alert and a Securité message on the VHF radio. It's important to do this first, before the water level rises enough to short out your batteries. Your hand-held VHF radio's range will be much less.

Next, pull up the sole boards in the main fore-and-aft passage to expose the length of the bilge and check to see if water is flooding in. If it is, make a note of its general direction of flow, or check for changes in boat trim, and you'll have a good idea of where to start looking for the leak. It's most likely to be forward.

Empty lockers until you find the hole. If you have clear access, and the hole isn't too big, stuff a cushion over it and hold it in place with your foot. This worked surprisingly well for us as a first response. If access is poor, clear any joinery with a hammer, then use the cushion. Now call your crew, assess the situation and plan what to do next.

Send a VHF radio DSC alert before the batteries are under water

Lift the sole board to see where the water is coming from

10 'Buy-you-time' repairs
As soon as you've located the hole, you can take steps to stop the water coming in

1 Cushion stamped against the hole

As the boat was lowered and the water began to gush in, my first reaction was a sudden rush of adrenalin. I grabbed a bright orange cushion, with a waterproof nylon cover, which I found in the forepeak and held it over the hole with my boot. This took a second and greatly reduced the flow of water. It was a major confidence boost and definitely the quickest quick fix.

It's fast and effective but what's your next move?

2 Flat plywood board

This involved using a coat hanger to push a loop of line out through the hole, which a crewman on deck snagged with his boathook. He then inserted the line through a pre-drilled bunkboard, knotting the end to hold it in place, before I hauled the board from inside the boat, tight against the outside of the hull. A G-clamp proved invaluable, providing a convenient anchor to tension the lines in this and other methods of stemming the flood. It took a couple of minutes to implement and the results weren't spectacular.

1. We poked out our hauling line using a straightened coat hanger

2. Kieran snagged the hauling line with a boathook and tied on the board

3. Even hauled in tight, this repair leaked quite badly

3 Flat engineroom board

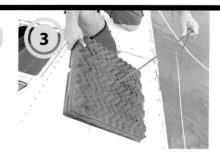

A piece of engineroom hatch, lined with sound-proofing sponge, was pre-drilled as the Mark II version of the flat plywood board solution. Once again, a loop of line was pushed through the hole, which Kieran, on deck, snagged with a boathook and inserted through the board's pre-drilled hole. It took the same time to deploy, but was much more effective.

1. We could have stamped a cushion over the hole while running the hauling line to our man on the outside

2. The hauling line was threaded through the board and fastened with a stopper knot before being hauled tight to cover the leak

3. With the board in place and the line secured and tightened used a G-clamp, we had a much more effective repair

4 Fothering a sail

Tried and trusted by Admiral Nelson after cannon ball damage, this involved wrapping a sail around the hull, leech forward as it's smoother. It was not quick. Lines needed attaching to each corner, then it needed a boathook to sink the sail under the hull's knuckle. Twists needed to be removed before see-sawing the sail into place and securing very tightly to the toerail. Sadly, due to the sail's built-in camber, it 'pulsed' against the hull, proving a decent fix one second, awful the next.

The sail 'pulsed' against the hull, making a bad repair one minute...

Fothering a sail took a long time and any sail is fundamentally ill-suited for the job

... and a pretty decent one the next. The result isn't worth the time

5 DIY collision mat

I tried to get a purpose-made collision mat, priced at £622 ($999), from an American company, but they never replied, so I spent £16.99 on a sheet of damp-course membrane and £17 on four Strong Grips (clips). If not pre-prepared, it takes five minutes to assemble, longer than preparing the sail. It also needed to be prodded under the hull's knuckle, but the flat, smooth material was see-sawed into place more easily than the sail and sat flat on the hull, stopping the torrent of water almost completely.

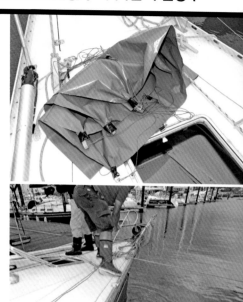

STRONG GRIPS
Available from Swedish company Aronowitsch and Lyth. For the nearest dealer visit their website: www.arolyth.se

6 Lifejacket wrapped in a towel

The assembly needed shoving through the hole

It reduced flow significantly but opened up splits around the hole

This idea really appealed to me – fast and ingenious. At least, it might have been, with a bigger, rounder hole. As it was, I needed to stuff the assembly through the hole with an oar, making the hole bigger and the gush of water worse. Once in place, I fired the manual inflator and the flood slowed considerably. However, the inflation did open splits in the hull and water seeped relentlessly through them.

It's ready in seconds and it's appealingly simple

7 Umbrella

Always a bit of a long shot, this one, but worth trying if only to challenge the old truism about the two most useless things aboard a yacht being a retired Navy officer and an umbrella. This one was a giveaway brolly from a newspaper promotion. I tied a line to the tip (to make sure the umbrella didn't sink into the marina) and then prodded it through the hole. When I tried to open the brolly, the handle fell off inside the hull. Looking at the shreds caused by the splintered GRP, it wouldn't have worked anyway.

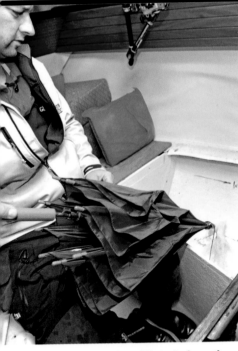

With the retrieval line tied on, the brolly was ready to go

It wasn't easy to push it through the hole

It worked for Mary Poppins, but not for us

8 Subrella

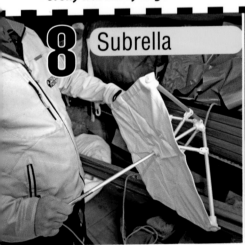

The Subrella is no longer made. Production volumes were not high enough to bring down costs

The Subrella was too big for our hole and needed forcing through with an oar

The Subrella made the hole bigger but slowed the flood of water substantially

This is a purpose-made emergency collision 'patch' – a sort of hi-tech 'umbrella'. As before, a line was tied on to prevent loss before it was thrust through the hole. Because of the size of the Subrella and the relatively small hole, it had to be hammered through with the blunt end of an oar. The hole was enlarged as a result but, once deployed with its safety line secured to the G-clamp, it slowed the flood to a level that would definitely buy you time. Alas, it is no longer in production and the patent belongs to a now defunct company.

9 Towel in garden refuse bag

This idea aimed to exploit external water pressure by forcing a bagged item through the hole so that the water pressure could force it back against the hole, sealing it. Unfortunately, the bag shredded as it was pushed through the jagged hole, leaving the towel prising the hole open and allowing water to gush in. It wasn't an encouraging result and we perhaps overestimated the water pressure.

Quickly and easily prepared, but does it work in practice?

No, it simply made the hole bigger

10 Sail in sailbag

The principle was to push the sail bag through the hole then stuff the cruising chute into the external part of the bag so the water pressure could push it back onto the hull. We overestimated the water pressure and this method simply forced the GRP shards apart and made the hole bigger. The flood of water can only be estimated from what was flowing out of the bulkhead, but it wasn't encouraging.

Another simple idea, but does it work in practice?

No, the hole bigger simply got bigger

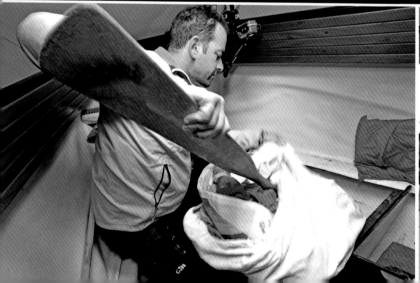

1

5 'Get-you-home' repairs
You saved the boat; can you improve it and get home?

Having established that our best 'quick fix' to stop the leak was the DIY collision mat, we had bought ourselves some time to test more permanent repairs to get your boat back in harbour.

1. The collision mat
2. Braced board and cushion
3. A sheet of 2mm plywood coated with mastic and grease, braced against the hull
4. The same sheet fastened to the hull with self-tapping screws
5. Underwater epoxy repair kit

With the collision mat stemming the flow of water we tried each method, removing the mat to see how well they worked. At sea, there would be no obvious reason to remove the mat, but unless you get a tight seal at the sheet's leading edge, it's unlikely to last long once the yacht is underway. Covering the plastic sheet with a fothered sail would protect it from the waves, improving its durability.

1 DIY collision mat

We wanted to test how watertight the DIY mat would be with the yacht underway. Since the Crash Test Boat had no working engine or rig we asked the travel hoist crew to move the boat ahead and astern in the slings. While the mat had been effective in the earlier test, it leaked badly on this occasion. In a real-life situation you will have no choice but to persist and get this right if you can't access the hole from inside the hull. We believe it's a method that can work.

3

2

1. Position the mat correctly and you can almost seal the hole

2. The DIY collision mat made from a damp course membrane

3. The collision mat needed persuasion to position it under the hull's knuckle

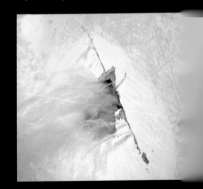

Our second attempt with the collision mat leaked when we simulated the yacht being underway

2 Braced board and cushion

It was difficult to shape the cushion to the hole. A thinner pillow worked better, but we didn't have a bracing board small enough for the orange pillow. Nor could we find a brace strong enough to exert sufficient pressure. The deck broom was about to break so we used the boathook, which did break. We could have sawn the spinnaker pole, but to what length? Could we deploy it in such a confined space? Given plenty of time, it would have worked but the clock was ticking and we needed to try other methods.

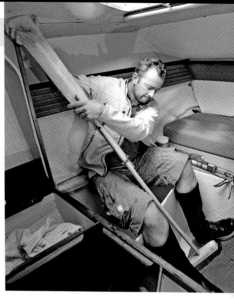

Bracing seems an obvious solution but in practice we struggled to make it work

Two items hose-clipped together make an adjustable brace

3 Braced, bonded board

We slapped half a tub of Ramonol marine grease around the hole and squeezed a ring of fast-curing mastic onto one side of a 2mm marine plywood board. The plan was to brace this board over the hole using a cushion and bracing board, with the grease making a quick seal while the mastic cured to provide a more lasting seal. Unfortunately, due to the bracing problems described, we never exerted the pressure required, the leak never stopped and the mastic never cured. Solve the bracing issue and this might work.

We put grease around the hole and a ring of mastic on the board

Even with a decent brace, the cushion softened the force

Bad bracing and poor curing conditions scuppered this idea

4 Bonded and fastened board

We tried nailing the same 2mm ply board in place, still covered in grease and mastic, but it was impossible to penetrate the hull. Self-tapping screws also did not work. We used a double-pinion hand drill because a battery electric one underwater wouldn't work. Despite breaking a drill bit, we made five holes and, using the self-tapping screws, secured a 2mm ply board over the hole. It worked well. Despite the grease, the board was beginning to 'sweat' after five minutes, so thicker, but still flexible ply, would be a better option.

1. Drilling holes in the hull wasn't easy with a hand drill but we eventually managed it

2. We used five self-tapping screws to secure the board

3. Self-tappers held the board well but water was starting to 'sweat' through it

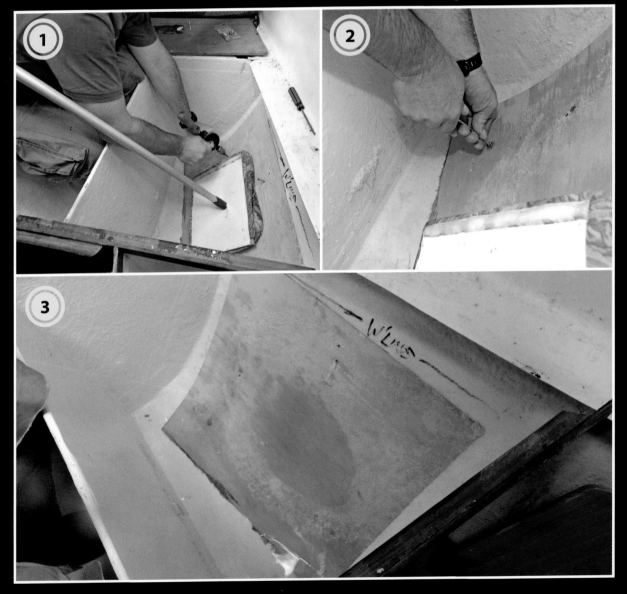

5 Epoxy repair kit

The Kollision Kit is an underwater repair kit with a two-pack epoxy bonding system promising rapid cure. Having keyed the surface with the wet-and-dry sandpaper supplied, I cut the mat to fit, mixed the two epoxy parts, spread the epoxy on the polymat and placed it over the hole. Having braced it in place for five minutes, it created a very decent repair. Under time pressure, I couldn't mix all the epoxy, as it was difficult to spoon out of the pots, so I didn't get the coverage I needed and, after a couple of minutes, a small leak appeared. In general, though malodorous and messy, it was very easy to apply.

Price £71 Contact Epoxy Solutions Tel 01454 612445
Website www.epoxysolutions.co.uk

Scoop out and mix the two parts of epoxy using the wooden spatula

Smear the mixed epoxy on the furry side of the polymat supplied

Then, with the fother in place, put the mat over the hole

Brace the repair against the hull for five minutes while the epoxy cures

What we learned

> *There's every reason to suggest that not only can you keep her afloat, you could even bail her dry*

YOU CAN SAVE YOUR BOAT

Being holed below the waterline presents a number of problems in a variety of scenarios, depending on the size and location of the hole, but you can almost certainly save your boat. During this test, a very clear action plan emerged and, with a few inexpensive, multi-purpose preparations such as the DIY collision mat and Strong Grips, a hand drill, some self-tapping screws, and the Kollision Kit, which can also be used for other repairs, there's every reason to suggest that not only can you keep her afloat, you could even bail her dry.

THE QUICKEST FIX

Stamping a soft cushion (ours had a Nylon waterproof cover) over the hole took a fraction of a second and stemmed the flooding very well. It would be my first response, to buy time. Some cushions are too resistant to taking up the shape of the hole, as are sailbags. If you can brace the cushion in place, you'll be free to move around, but we struggled to make bracing work. If you can't access the hole from inside the yacht, move straight to the next step and get a sail or collision mat in place on the outside of the hull.

A cushion over the hole was fast and effective, but you can't move until you find a brace

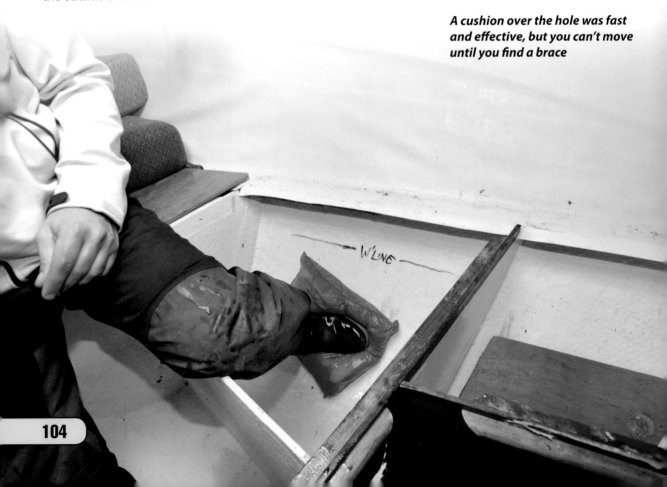

We used a damp course with Strong Grips (clips) and mousing twine to haul it into place. On reflection, I'd use a thicker line because the sheet needs to be taut and mousing twine cuts into the hands and is difficult to tie securely. We discovered Strong Grips on sale at Southampton Boat Show. They're supposed to be used for holding awnings and covers in place, but I thought they'd be ideal for this purpose. A waterproof tarpaulin would work instead of damp course, and it would have cringles already fitted.

If you're holed either side of a fin keel, or you have a long-keeler, you'll need to position the sheet on the damaged side of the centreline. Tie off the fore and aft upper lines to the toerail at a diagonal angle.
With a fin-keeler, run the lower lines under the bow and stern, using a boathook to poke the aft line under the rudder and secure them on the opposite toerail.

If you have a long-keeler, run the aft line under the counter and up to the opposite stern fairlead and the forward line under the bow and up to the opposite fairlead, and tie both off. Water pressure should take care of the rest, but be ready to seesaw the sheet into place and check below to see if it's working.

What you need onboard

Our plan was to only use kit that you might find on the average cruising yacht. By and large, we managed to stick to our plan. One exception was the hand drill. We were lifting the yacht in the Travelhoist and draining the hull between each repair method so we could assess the effectiveness of each test before the internal water level rose above the hole. At sea that's not an option and it's likely you will be working underwater, so an electric drill won't work. Trying to hammer nails into GRP proved futile, so we spent £5.95 on a hand drill. It wasn't easy to use, but eventually we succeeded.

' Seesaw the plastic sheet into place and check below to see if it works '

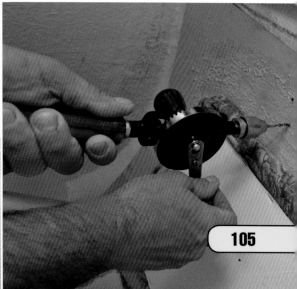

We practised placing the DIY collision mat on dry land

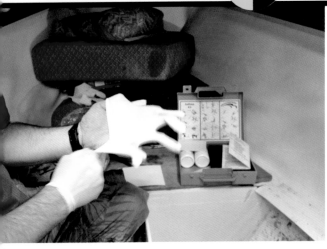

Another exception was the epoxy repair kit. We had the perfect opportunity to test the Kollision Kit. It comes in a plastic case from Epoxy Solutions, a UK company. The Royal Marines, among others, use the kit to repair beach-damaged RIB hulls. It's intended for external application, but I would never recommend readers leap overboard. Applying the required pressure around the repair outside would also be problematic. It can't be used if water is flooding in, but as the collision mat had worked so well, reducing flow to almost nothing, we thought it was worth a shot.

Two tips: The rubber gloves supplied took ages to haul on, finger by finger. Use washing-up gloves instead. Secondly, the two epoxy parts ought to be supplied in tubes or syringes. With the adrenalin pumping, I wasn't keen to fiddle around with the wooden spatulas that were supplied, spooning out every last bit of epoxy. Unfortunately, when spreading it onto the polymat, I didn't have enough to cover the edges completely and that's where the leak appeared. My mistake, but I'm sure it wouldn't be an uncommon one.

12 minutes to sink a 30ft yacht...

We had an 8cm (3in) hole 20cm (8in) below the waterline. It may not have looked too threatening but in the first 7–8 minutes of the test, of which maybe 30 seconds was spent with nothing covering the hole, displacement increased by 2,000kg, suggesting 2,000 litres (440 gallons) had leaked in. The water was 5cm (2in) above the sole and 20cm (8in) above the bilge. When holed, response speed is of the essence.

Flow rate mathematics is quite complicated but the estimates I found suggest that a 5cm (2in) hole 30cm (1ft) below the waterline will leak 300 litres (66 gallons) per minute. A 10cm (4in) hole at the same depth leaks 1,100 litres (242 gallons) per minute, enough to sink a 30ft yacht in 12 minutes.

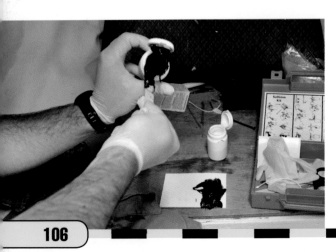

In a test of 16 hand-operated bilge pumps, the number of litres bailed out by a man with a bucket was the second fastest method – even up against the formidable power of a Whale Gusher pump

1. This small hole let in 2,000 litres in 7–8 minutes

2. It's difficult to believe this small leak could have sunk our yacht in 30 minutes

3. Panic tends to rise with the water level but it's important to think clearly

How we sank our yacht 10 times

This test required repeated 'sinkings' to assess the effectiveness of various repair methods, so we decided to 'sink' the boat using the slings of MDL's Hamble Point Marina travel hoist. We lifted and drained the hull between each test to assess how effective each method had been. Had we not done this, the hole would soon have been below water, making this difficult.

TWO-STAGE TESTING
First, we explored emergency measures to stop the flood, buy time and regain control. For these, we used kit you would expect to find on an average cruising yacht. Then we tried out some ideas for making good a longer-lasting repair that would have enabled us to sail home – hopefully without continual pumping and bailing.

We chose to smash a hole in the hull under the forecabin bunk on the starboard side. To improve access for filming and photography, we removed both heads doors and the pillar between.

This had the benefit of making the hole fairly easy to get at. At sea, it's quite possible that the hole would have straddled and partially destroyed a bulkhead. While the bulkhead would be easy enough to clear, the lamination at its joints would not, making any internal repair very tricky. In that instance, an external method of stopping the flood should buy enough time for a longer-term repair below.

MAKING THE HOLE
With the boat in a cradle, yacht repair company Osmotech UK set to work smashing the hole in the hull, which proved amazingly strong! The area inside the hull was first weakened by an angle-grinder, followed by 25 minutes of bashing with a lump-hammer. Finally, we had a hole roughly 8cm (3in) across, around 20cm (8in) below the waterline. The GRP shards were pushed into the boat to simulate collision damage. To drain the bilge between tests, we drilled two 5cm (2in) holes either side of the keel, through inch-thick laminate, using circular drill bits. During tests, these were plugged from inside with wooden bungs.

We had no idea what to expect, so our tests were carried out with the boat held safely in the travel hoist's slings

Osmotech's man started battering the hull with a 12lb lump hammer...

The hull's resistance to being whacked with a 12lb hammer was impressive, but a moving 7-tonne boat striking a rock would result in a quite different outcome. We also knocked out some interior joinery in the forward cabin, to avoid concerns that water would flood only that sector to the waterline, then stop. This also allowed us to better assess how much water was flooding in – and demonstrated how easy it is to smash away interior woodwork to access a hole. Very easy, except for the lamination point at the hull.

The test was as valid as any of this type could be. After a collision, no two holes will be the same. Each will present different challenges but meeting them will require similar methods. We tested many ways to stop water flooding into the hull, some of which only occurred to us on the day. The big surprise was that, even with a small hole, in just seven minutes we had two tonnes of water inside the hull.

REAL LIFE STORY

Sunk in the North Sea

Dutch sailor Menko Poen and his son Victor abandoned their 32ft yacht when she sank after a mystery collision 25 miles north-east of Ramsgate. They were adrift in their liferaft for eight hours in the English Channel

My son Victor (13) and I set sail from Lowestoft one afternoon in June heading for Ramsgate, on our way to the Scilly Isles, where the rest of the family planned to join us for a holiday. Our yacht, *Laughing Gull III*, was a 32ft GRP fin-keeled boat, built in 1981 in Amsterdam.

The weather was a squally SW Force 6 to 7, veering and easing to westerly Force 5. Keeping clear of sandbanks in the Thames Estuary, I plotted our position on the chart regularly and although it was wet and windy and hard work in the squalls, it was also exhilarating sailing.

We were 25 miles north-east of Ramsgate and I was on watch, while Victor rested in his bunk below,

when at around at 0130BST, I heard a bumping sound and the boat's speed dropped. She was also pushed to port. Although this seemed consistent with the conditions, I felt something was wrong.

I turned my head and listened, waiting for the sound to come again. But it didn't. I leaned through the companionway and asked Victor if he had noticed anything. He told me he'd heard a sound like a loud knock on a door. He'd also noticed we were pushed to port.

Still not sure what had happened, I checked the bilges and saw to my horror they were full of water. I couldn't see any damage and the keel bolts seemed fine. Soon the water level was above the floor and, despite bailing with a bucket, it continued to rise, pouring into my boots. I checked the seacocks. If something was wrong with them, I could stop the flow with a wooden plug. But they were OK.

This meant there must be damage to the hull itself. I continued bailing and considered pulling a sail around the outside of the hull to try and stem the flood. But with a fin keel, it was unlikely I'd get the sail close enough to the hull to have any effect. I thought of breaking off the cupboards and interior fittings to inspect the hull for damage, but the water was pouring in so fast, there wasn't time.

By now, water was up to my knees and rising. I told Victor we had to abandon the yacht. I stressed there was nothing to be afraid of and discussed what had to be done: sending out a Mayday, firing flares (if appropriate) and preparing the liferaft.

I didn't want to go on deck to lower the sails in case this caused the boat to capsize. I trimmed the sails so the movements were steady. I sent Victor into the cockpit to help stabilise the yacht and started to send the first Mayday on VHF Channel 16. I had an instruction booklet handy to remind me of the procedure. I also had the ship's name written out in the phonetic alphabet.
I transmitted 5 to 10 Maydays, but with no response. By now, I realised, the batteries were completely underwater. As I was transmitting the last Mayday, the water was up to my chest as I sat at the chart table, and the switchboard was half underwater. Before I left the cabin, I wrote on a piece of paper that the crew had abandoned the sinking yacht and were all OK – in case *Laughing Gull III* was found afloat.

I carried the liferaft from the front cabin, wading through the water in the saloon, into the cockpit. On the horizon, I spotted two ships. I fired two parachute flares and lit one red hand-flare. Although I estimated the ships were only a few miles away, they didn't respond. Not all our hand and parachute flares worked, although they were almost brand new.

We deployed the liferaft, after carefully studying the instructions. We tied it to the stern and dropped it

overboard, yanking the rope to activate automatic inflation when it was about 10m away. We pulled the raft against the stern and I told Victor to jump – but safely! A horrifying moment it was! Then I followed Victor, remembering the phrase: 'Only use your liferaft when the step into it is a step upwards!' I can assure readers that we were just in time!

The only things we took with us were two torches, a knife, my passport and credit cards. Everything else we left behind.

At 0210 BST we cut the liferaft loose from *Laughing Gull III* – an emotional moment as it meant a final goodbye to my yacht. Until then, I was still hoping for rescue by a lifeboat or any other vessel with an electrical pump. The weather was fair: it was dry, the wind was westerly Force 5, with good visibility and a moon shining through the clouds. I remember thinking it was beautiful sailing weather.

It was almost high water and the tide was soon going to turn with the north-going ebb. Taking into account the tide and our approximate position, I realised we were slowly drifting towards the Traffic Separation Scheme (TSS). I looked back at *Laughing Gull III* and could still see her masthead light. Just before sunrise the light suddenly disappeared, meaning that she had sunk, or the batteries had gone dead.

In the liferaft it was cold, with a water temperature of only 9°C. Keeping up our morale was my number one priority. I was completely soaked and my muscles were aching. I was also very tired, but I was still capable of thinking clearly. Victor was in a bad condition and was severely seasick and unable to swallow water. He had to pee and he asked me where he should do that. I told him I had just done so myself a moment ago in my trousers and the warmth on my legs had been very welcome to me. We both tried to sleep for a while or at least closed our eyes.

When we noticed vessels in our vicinity, we fired red parachutes and hand flares. Although the ships were close – we could see their navigation lights reflected in the water – they didn't respond. After sunrise, more ships in the TSS became visible. They were moving to the SW and, as the wind was blowing us to the east, there was a risk of being run down.

I looked at the liferaft's solitary paddle, which was very small. I decided to wait until the ebb, which would push us in a N to NE direction. By paddling, with the help of tide and wind, I hoped we could move to the NE, alongside the TSS. I calculated that the ebb would start running again at about 1400. So, I still had time to rest. Then I heard an aeroplane above us. I regretted that I hadn't had time to grab our emergency bag with the orange dye. It would have coloured the water to draw the aircraft's attention. I also missed a mirror to give light-signals to ships. A handheld VHF would have been useful, too. Most of the time I kept a lookout with one of my hands holding Victor's ankle to reassure him I was there.

The silhouettes of the ships in the TSS were visible for some time when I saw a dot on the horizon slowly becoming a vertical line, then changing into two larger lines and finally transforming in three larger lines. It was a ship with three masts, slowly heading SW and closer than all other vessels. This could be our opportunity!
We still had left one red hand flare, two orange smoke signals and three white parachute flares. I reasoned that I had to wait until the ship was close enough but, on the other hand, our liferaft still had to be visible when looking ahead from the ship's bridge. I waited for the right moment before using our last two orange smoke signals and our last red hand flare.

Almost immediately after using the red hand flare we saw the ship's three masts becoming one. The ship had turned in our direction! We were saved and we embraced each other! After eight hours adrift in our liferaft, we were taken onboard the Norwegian Tall Ship *Sørlandet* on her way to Dunkirk at 1010. Dover Coastguard and the French authorities were informed. Victor and I were offered hot drinks and a meal, dry clothes and even a bunk, but, above all, a lot of understanding, warmth and kindness. Later, the crew of the *Sørlandet* told me that they could smell but not see the smoke from our flares, being on our leeside.

LESSONS LEARNED

- Be mentally prepared for shipwreck. Do not panic. Be prepared for failures, but maintain morale.
- Have the VHF Mayday-procedure at hand, including your ship's name in the phonetic alphabet.
- Being able to drop the mainsail and take all speed off the yacht might have reduced the flood of water.
- Make sure you have your emergency grab bag in a place where it can be easily found. We left ours behind, with its orange dye and signalling mirror. A handheld VHF would have been useful, too.
- Have the liferaft stowed on deck, if possible, or in the cockpit or a locker. Stowing it in the forward cabin is not the best place, in case of collision. There might not be time to carry it through the saloon in case of fire aboard.
- Reading the instructions for deploying your liferaft when you are abandoning ship is not the best time! Find time to rehearse your emergency procedures on a normal sailing outing.
- Make sure you have wooden plugs tied to the seacocks and they are the right size.
- Make sure your bilge pump is not blocked by debris.
- Do you have an emergency kit aboard so you can make provisional repairs of the hull?
- Don't count too much on VHF Ch 16. These days a DSC VHF is better. And an EPIRB (Electronic Position Indicating Radio Beacon) is even better. A Search and Rescue Transponder (SART) also improves your chances of detection by SAR.
- Even with just two of us, we found space in the four-man liferaft limited and suffered cramp and fatigue.

Menko Poen is a 49-year-old physician who extensively cruised the North Sea, the Channel and the Baltic, mostly singlehanded.

This first-hand account is taken from Total Loss, an anthology of 38 disasters at sea edited by Paul Gelder (Adlard Coles Nautical)

Sunk by a UFO – Unidentified Floating Object

A spur of the moment decision to go for a sail ended in disaster for Peter Jackson when his yacht hit a submerged object and began to sink

I was heading out into Plymouth Sound for a short sail. There was a fresh breeze from the north-west but the sea remained fairly calm. *Yondi*, a T24, was a small boat with a fin keel capable of deep sea sailing. She was a home away from the stress of work for my wife and myself and we had explored nearly all the deep-water harbours and anchorages from Dartmouth to the Isles of Scilly and across to the Channel Islands.

Soon we were flying along at nearly 7 knots on the way to the Eddystone Lighthouse when suddenly, there was a tremendous crash and I was thrown forward. I thought we must have collided with another vessel, but nothing was in sight and I knew there were no rocks in the vicinity. Then I saw a huge log, about 30ft long and around 5ft in diameter, covered in weed and goose barnacles. It was floating just under the waves.

I went below to look for damage and was surprised I could find no damage, except for a slight seepage into the bilge which the electric pump could deal with. I dropped sail and started the engine to motor home. After about 10 minutes water reached the top of the sump, so I started using the bilge pump. I guessed water was seeping up around the keelbolts, which had been loosened by the impact. The water level rose steadily and I was no longer able to keep pace. Then matters took a turn for the worse. As water reached the lower lockers labels were washed off tinned food and sucked into the pump strainer. I cleared it several times, but it blocked almost immediately. The water level rose quickly and when it reached up to my waist as the boat rolled, I broadcast a 'Mayday' call on the VHF radio.

I was five miles south of the western end of Plymouth Breakwater. The Coastguard told me help was on its way. I put my lifejacket on and went to inflate my dinghy on the foredeck. I'd just started inflating it when the lifeboat called to obtain a radio fix on my position.

Floating logs as well as shipping containers are hidden hazards at sea

The cabin was now a dangerous place. Every time *Yondi* rolled, floating debris was being thrown around the cabin.

The first help to arrive was a fast RIB from Fort Bovisand Diving Centre with three fit young men on board. They were soon bailing with buckets. The lifeboat arrived and brought a large petrol pump over to *Yondi* by dinghy. However, the lifeboat men couldn't start the pump. It was decided to bring the lifeboat alongside and use its bigger pump. I was just taking the hose from a crew member when the coxswain ordered us all to leave *Yondi*. No one moved. The order was repeated in stronger, louder language! This convinced us. Somehow my lifejacket got entangled with one of the backstays and for what seemed a lifetime I was firmly attached to the boat. Eventually, I freed myself and jumped into the sea just in time to see the top of the mast and the new, expensive furling foresail disappearing under the water. I remember thinking that I'd hardly used that sail. *Yondi* sank like a stone, leaving just a few pieces of debris floating on the surface. Even the partially inflated dinghy which had been untied did not appear. There was nothing to show that my beautiful boat had ever existed. I was soon on board the lifeboat being given a hot drink. The crew were embarrassed about not being able to start the pump but we all know that any mechanical item can always fail at a critical time.

*This first-hand account is taken from **Total Loss**, edited by Paul Gelder (Adlard Coles Nautical)*

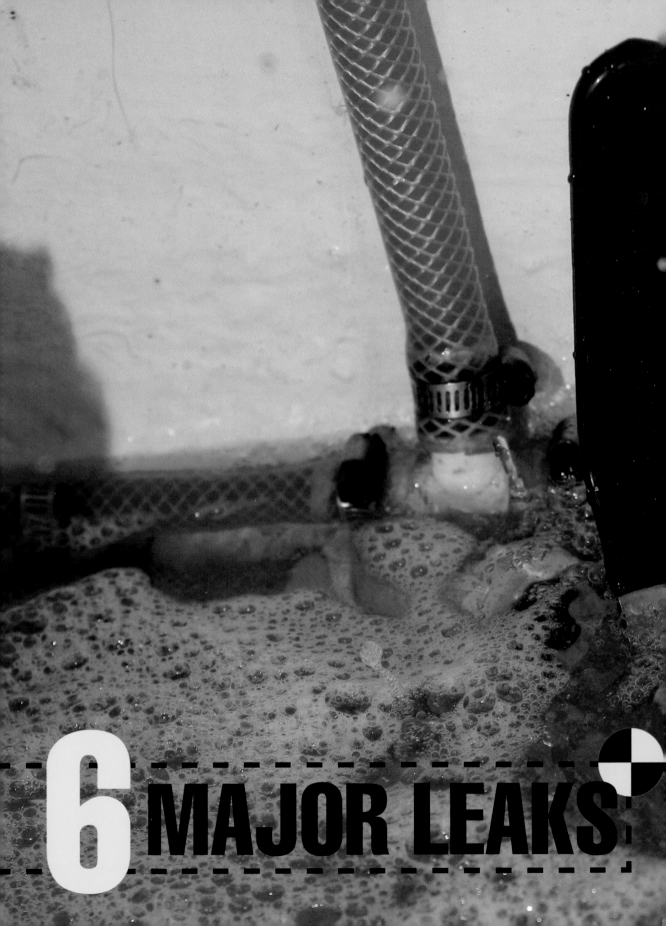

6 MAJOR LEAKS

What's the best way stop a hull leak?

Holes below the waterline are essential for plumbing, propulsion and engine cooling systems but intuitively they're not a good idea. In 2011, *Yachting Monthly* launched a seacock safety campaign following warnings from a leading marine surveyor who was telling yachtsmen that their boats could be in danger of sinking because thousands of seacocks and through-hull fittings are made from brass rather than bronze.

This seacock sheared off at the skin fitting, leaving a leaking hole that could have sunk the yacht

Paul Stevens, 59, a founding member of British Marine Surveyors Europe, was 'incredulous' that some boatbuilders were fitting out yachts with brass ball valve-type seacocks designed for fresh water plumbing and piping systems. We invited Paul, a marine surveyor with 20 years' experience and the whistleblower for seacock safety, to be our consultant for this test.

Paul explained the nightmare lottery of seacock safety and the fact that in salt water brass is prone to a form of corrosion called dezincification, which makes them brittle and subject to failure. 'It used to be the case that boatbuilders only ever fitted bronze seacocks which are virtually fail-safe,' he said. But bronze and DZR brass – which is resistant to corrosion – is four times the price of ordinary brass. Ironically, the European Community's Recreational Craft Directive of 1998 made the situation worse with its ISO standard for metallic seacocks and through-hull fittings which states they should be

corrosion-resistance for a service time of five years.

'A five-year service life is not acceptable for crucial fit-and-forget below-the-waterline fitting,' said Paul, who explained that seacocks have three failure modes. The most common is where a corroded pipe shears off at the hull, leaving nothing more than a hole. The second is when the ball valve cracks, leaving just the through-hull fitting. In the third failure scenario, the hose slips off the tail pipe inboard of the ball valve, or the corroded tail pipe disintegrates following a slight knock, but the ball valve is jammed and can't be closed.

Log and echo-sounder transducer fittings can fail, too. Often the internal securing nut is mounted on a wooden pad. If it's not installed properly, the wood can get wet and swell, shearing the nut off the thread, which means the fitting can fall out of the boat. If, as on the Crash Test Boat, the fitting is on a sharp turn of the bilge, the outer flange isn't supported across its full diameter and can crack. When the flange breaks, the internal fitting is fired into the boat by the water pressure. Another possibility is that the internal securing nut is overtightened, which can also lead to cracking and a similar result.

All manufacturers recommend the internal nut, once tightened, is covered with a fillet of epoxy or FRP paste that spreads onto the hull. Should the outer flange fail, the fillet will prevent the entire fitting from being pushed into the boat. However, Paul says that on 90 per cent of the boats he has surveyed, it hasn't been done.

Failure of a through-hull fitting demands urgent attention. While seacocks can fail without anyone aboard, it's often the human touch that finally precipitates failure by operating a ball valve or knocking a tail pipe. These are the scenarios we wanted to recreate and, in each of these cases, we tested the received wisdom and tried out a few methods suggested by readers, too.

How long will your seacocks last?

This test is based on the assumption that you are on the boat and able to do something about a through-hull failure. Unfortunately, through-hulls are just as likely to fail when you're not aboard. That's why *Yachting Monthly* launched its seacock safety campaign in a bid to change the European Recreational Craft Directive five-year standard and persuade boatbuilders and chandleries to disclose and label more clearly what sort of seacocks they fit and sell, and to ensure that customers are offered the choice of longer-lasting fittings, like bronze or plastic.

Several yacht surveyors and owners have shared horror stories about boats that nearly sank because of unsuitable brass seacocks below the waterline. Chandleries, too, have admitted it's difficult to establish the metal content of what they are ordering, especially when fittings are often unmarked or poorly labelled.

The Marine Accident Investigation Board made strong recommendations following the sinking of a vessel due to the failure of Tonval brass fittings below the waterline. Their report stated that the use of brass below the waterline neither meets ISO 9093 or the RCD.

Nigel Calder, the world's foremost expert on boat systems told *YM*: 'I have raised concerns for several years about the through-hull fittings on a number of new boats, especially those manufactured in Europe, many of which appear to use some form of plated brass and not bronze. This concern was recently reinforced by a through hull tailpipe on a two-year-old boat with a leaking hairline fracture. On investigation, the fitting was found to be almost corroded through. It could easily have broken off and sunk the boat. A through-hull fitting is essentially an extension of the hull. It needs the same integrity as the hull for the life of the boat. In terms of metal fittings, only high quality bronze is suitable.'

Check which type of metal your seacocks are made from. Get professional advice if necessary. And service your seacocks when you lay up. In doing so, you'll become familiar with where they are and how easy they are to get at, and you'll discover any problems before they occur. Replace them with proper DZR or bronze if there's the slightest sign of weakness.

CONCLUSION
Beware the vast majority of silver coloured ball valves with red handles. Most are ordinary brass. In the absence of electrolytic action, they may be alright. But none measure up to the standard of DZR so why take the risk? DZR and bronze (Blakes seacocks) are approved. Anything else, apart from Marelon plastic seacocks, is suspect.

Photo credit: Kieran Flatt

The Test: Commercial Products

SOFTWOOD BUNG

A selection of bungs cost from £9 at various chandlers

Everyone has wooden bungs aboard, or should have. It's an inexpensive solution to a potentially disastrous problem, but is it an effective one? The answer is yes. A bung is quick and easy to deploy and has no moving parts or breakable elements. With an intact log transducer through-hull fitting, we didn't need to use much force to insert the bung and it formed a perfect seal.

With a damaged pipe, insertion was just as easy but the seal was imperfect and a small fountain of water jetted out of the forward edge of the pipe.

With the log transducer fitting knocked off at hull level, the bung once again formed a perfect seal, leaving no doubt that, in this scenario, the bung would give you control of the situation and would save the boat.

The bung was also effective with the seacock tail pipe, but noticeably less so. Paul pointed out that it's not rare for the tail pipe to break in the way ours did, distorting the pipe. The bung significantly reduced flooding but there was a steady stream of water pouring past the bung at the tear. Again, it would give you control of the situation but you would need to pump the bilges two or three times an hour while you're preparing a more effective repair. I found the bung difficult to extract, as it was jammed against the rough lining of the pipe. With a fragile pipe, obviously you need to be gentle removing the bung to avoid making the problem worse.

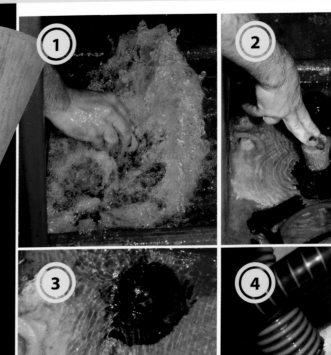

❝ A wooden bung is quick and easy to deploy and forms a perfect seal ❞

1. The most common solution is cheap, simple and quick to deploy if a through-hull breaks

2. With the fitting smashed away completely, leaving a round hole, the bung forms a perfect seal

3. It significantly reduces the leak but forms an imperfect seal if the tailpipe is cracked or deformed

4. With a cracked tailpipe, the bung leaves a fairly serious leak

(1)

FORESPAR TRUPLUG

Price £19.95
www.forespar.com

This hi-tech bung has a smooth, waterproof exterior
and a malleable, closed-cell polyurethane foam interio
It's quite a size, about 23x12cm (9x5in), but weighs
just 110g (4oz). That means it can plug holes of up
to 10cm (4in) and it's light enough not to fall out in a
seaway. Rather than just plugging into the pipe, you ar
supposed to grip the cone with one hand, the base wit
the other, and twist it in. It formed a perfect seal with
the damaged log pipe, stopping the leak completely.
With the log pipe knocked out to hull level, it was also
perfect fit.

With the broken seacock tail pipe, the TruPlug again made a
perfect seal but its size and the confines of the space meant
that pushing it into place took a moment longer than it might
have. It's worth noting that the manufacturers suggest slicing
the TruPlug to deal with hull splits so, if the space was seriously
confined, we could have sliced its nose off and pushed that
into the seacock. It sealed each leak perfectly and, like a bung,
there's very little that can go wrong with it, so it's well suited to
this task. The only issue, again, is the size. Stowing two TruPlugs
would take up considerably more space than two soft wood
bungs, and they're about £20 each, twice the price you'd pay fo
a bag of assorted soft wood bungs.

(2)

(3)

*1. The closed-cell foam
TruPlug is inserted using
a squeezing, twisting
and pushing action. It's
light, pliable and easily
manipulated*

*2. With a damaged log pipe,
the TruPlug formed a perfect
seal and stopped the leak
completely*

*3. With the fitting knocked
away the TruPlug also
formed a perfect seal,
stopping the leak*

*A perfect seal in the cracke
tailpipe, but TruPlug is very
big*

STAY AFLOAT

Price 400g (14oz) £24.99
www.stayafloatmarine.com

This by-product of petroleum production is described as a 'mouldable polymer'. When cold, it's similar to tepid wax in texture and, once out of the pot, can be worked fairly easily in the hand. I used this in the Sinking Crash Test to seal the 2mm (1/16in) holes we had drilled in the hull to fix a sheet of thin plywood over a big hole – and it worked perfectly. That said, a screw hole and a 40mm (1½in) seacock tailpipe are very different beasts.

After a couple of seconds spent scooping out enough of the gunge to stuff into the hole, I smeared the brown ball over the tail pipe and the flow stopped immediately. The advantage of this material over a soft wood bung is that it's amorphous, so it doesn't matter how distorted the tail pipe is, nor do you need to force it into the pipe, which could damage it further.

We removed the galley sink drain pipe and opened the seacock to create a gusher

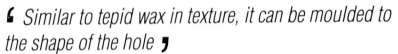

❝ *Similar to tepid wax in texture, it can be moulded to the shape of the hole* ❞

Its main drawback, based on the knowledge that the majority of broken seacocks snap off flush at the hull, is that it won't fair as well as a bung in that situation.

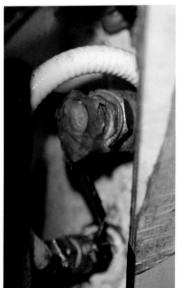

There wasn't much water pressure at the heads outlet, but we'd already destroyed the log pipe so I sought out a similar challenge for the gunk.

We removed the hose from the 40mm (1½in) galley sink drain outlet, at the lowest point in the boat and an impressive geyser shot up. This time, I simply upended the pot on the tailpipe, twisted the pot and then lifted it off. It stopped the leak completely.

Stay Afloat also sealed the cracked tailpipe, adapting to its irregular shape with ease

Faced with a serious leak, I stuck the pot over it, twisted and it sealed perfectly

The Test: Improvised Solutions

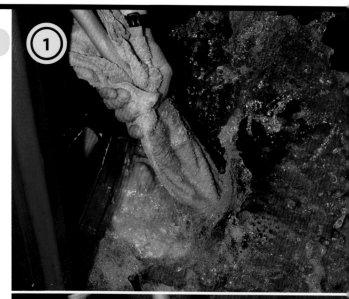

TOWEL

On finding a broken seacock or transducer, your first reaction would be to try and stop the spurting water with your hand – and that's a perfectly valid and effective first response, but it does rather limit your movement! We looked around the heads for something we could use to stem the flow other than a hand, and found a towel. We needed something to poke it into the hole with and that could have been a toothbrush or loo brush handle. We happened to have half of our broken boathook from a previous test, so we used that to stuff the towel into the log pipe.

The result was quite satisfactory. The flood of water stopped almost completely, which would restore your movement and buy you enough time to work out a better temporary repair. Obviously, within a minute or two the towel would become soaked and could well have succumbed to the water pressure and been pushed out of the hole. Having used it to shove the towel into the pipe, we removed the boathook but, as Paul pointed out, it could just as well be braced and left in place, improving the security of the repair. Greasing the towel would have improved the effectiveness of this method.

> ❛ It would buy you enough time to work out a better temporary repair ❜

1. There will always be a towel to hand which you can stuff into the hole

2. We used a boathook to push the towel in the hole

3. The towel stayed in place but it's a very temporary solution

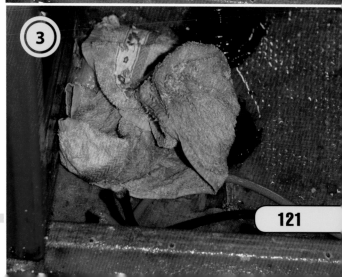

CARROT

Before embarking on this test we went on *Yachting Monthly*'s internet chat forum, Scuttlebutt, to ask how readers would deal with a broken through-hull. One of the reports, possibly apocryphal, mentioned a grandfather who had saved his ship by plunging a carrot into the hole left by a broken seacock. The idea appealed to us as eco-friendly, multi-purpose and, above all, cheap, so we gave it a go.

We used the carrot in the log transducer fitting and it stemmed the flow perfectly. Unfortunately, despite being a decent size, we couldn't retrieve it from the pipe and it was destroyed in the process of breaking the log pipe down to hull level. I have no doubt, however, that 'nature's bung' would have been just as effective as the softwood ones. It would also have the same drawbacks, in that it would be unable to form a perfect seal on a broken, deformed or distorted tail pipe, but it would significantly reduce flow and buy you the time you'd need to save your boat.

' *Nature's bung stemmed the flow of water perfectly* ,

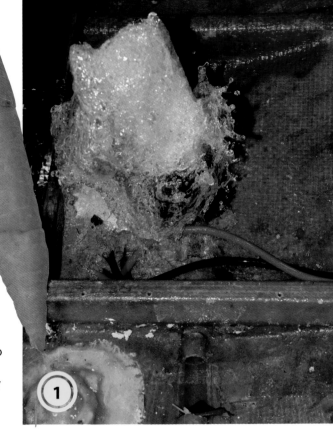

1. Water gushes in through the damaged log fitting

2. A suitably sized carrot is stuffed in the hole

3. I was expecting water pressure to eject the carrot

4. It fitted perfectly and stayed in position

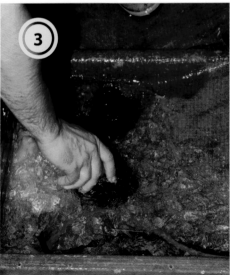

What we learned

' *Even a carrot and a potato stopped the leaks* ,

The good news is that there are many ways to seal a broken through-hull and most of them are significantly or completely successful. Stay Afloat and TruPlug worked perfectly, creating absolute seals, but the softwood bungs also stemmed the leaks very well. The jury is still out on where to stow wooden bungs – tied to the seacock, where they are instantly available, but could swell or split if left damp for long periods, or in a dry locker. They are inexpensive and effective solution.

So successful were the methods we tried that we didn't feel the need to test others – some of them rather bizarre – suggested by our readers. These included:

● Screwing an eye into a bung, poking a line out through the damaged through-hull, snagging it from the deck with a boathook, fastening the line to the bung and hauling it into place externally. We tried this briefly but, despite attaching a floating key fob to the line, it wouldn't surface from beneath the hull. This method might be more successful for a leak closer to the waterline.

● Cutting an inner tube, cable-tying one end over the broken through-hull, then raising the other end above sea level. We considered this but feared the torn tail pipe would rip the inner tube.

● Cutting a section of sea boot, greasing it, wrapping it over the broken through-hull and securing it in place with cable ties, hose clips, gaffer tape or self-fusing silicon tape.

● Putting a pork pie in a carrier bag and jamming it into the hole. After our experience with the towel in a bin bag in the sinking test, we believed the bag would shred and the pie would disintegrate, so we didn't try this one. There were other quicker, more reliable methods.

Don't panic – take control

Having re-created and lived through various potentially disastrous tests, several of the Crash Test Boat team have become inured to the drama and the sense of panic. It was chastening to see the reaction of our consultant, Paul Stevens, who confessed to a surge of adrenalin and a moment of panic as water gushed into the boat and quickly rose around his boots.

Panic is counterproductive in any of the Crash Test Boat scenarios. There are two main aims to the series: the first is to get you thinking about how you would tackle each situation yourself and what kit you could use. Secondly, we want to test all the methods suggested by received wisdom and secondhand experience, to see which works best and demonstrate how to deal with these situations as quickly and effectively as possible. Armed with the knowledge we have uncovered during this series, it is entirely possible that you can save your boat and your crew and make it back to safety. There is no need to panic.

A failed through-hull could sink your yacht, especially if you are not aboard

' *Armed with the knowledge from this chapter you can save your boat and crew* '

Man the bilge pumps

When you see the sole boards floating and the cabin awash, heave-to and get your crew to man the manual bilge pump. Next, check the water is salt and not from a fresh water tank failure – it would need to be a very large water tank to float the sole. Then check all your seacocks, ideally starting with the largest. Work out in advance which is the quickest circuit of your through-hulls and follow that. You'll be surprised how difficult some of them are to reach.

TRYING TO STOP THE LEAK
Having discovered which fitting is broken, get a hand to the through-hull and wedge something into the tail pipe. Then get the boat on the tack that gets the broken through-hull's inlet closest to or above the surface. Even if the problem is a detached hose, get something in the tail pipe so you have time to work out why the hose detached and whether it can be reattached.

Don't bother trying to strip out substantial sections of joinery to improve access because it will take too long. Our broken seacock was below the sink in the forward heads, so Paul tried to strip out the plywood sink unit with a hammer and a crowbar – it would be a tougher GRP moulding on newer boats – but after a minute, he had only removed the fascia.

Having bought yourself some time, pull up the sole boards and get your crew to start bailing into the galley sink, or the cockpit if it's self-draining. With a lot of water in the boat, there will be all sorts of debris floating around that will block the cockpit drains, and it's easier to clear if you're using the galley sinks. While they're doing that, return to the problem to see if you need to make a more durable repair, otherwise simply secure the one you have already put in place.

> *' There will be all sorts of debris that will block cockpit drains '*

1. First you have to track down the location of the leak

2. New boats have GRP mouldings, but even ply joinery wouldn't strip out

3. Paul tried to refit the outlet hose, but it wouldn't fit

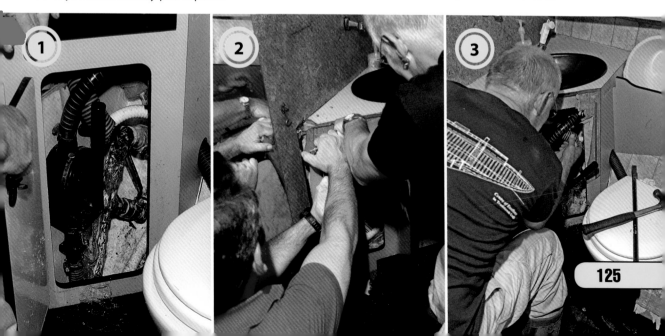

How did we do it?

Unless you are operating a seacock when it breaks, the first you will know about its failure is when you see the sole boards awash. This was not a scenario we wanted to recreate because if the seacocks or transducer fittings were submerged it would be impossible to evaluate the success of each repair method. So we called in an expert to help us – Paul Stevens, a founding member of British Marine Surveyors Europe. As with the previous sinking test, the Crash Test Boat was floating in MDL's travel hoist, at Hamble Point Marina, while we created and repaired holes. When the water rose above the fitting, we stopped testing so the hoist operator could lift the hull and drain it through two 2in holes drilled in the bilge.

For filming and photography we chose seacocks with good access. We chose the toilet outlet and log transducer in the forward heads, where both doors and a pillar between them had been removed. Starting with the log, we broke the fitting with a hammer, tried various methods of stemming the flow, then broke the internal securing nut to remove the fitting completely. We broke the nut, but the mastic used to secure it stopped us removing the fitting entirely. Using a hammer, we reduced it to hull level then tried various ways of stemming the flood.

For the second test, Paul removed the hose from the toilet outlet. Though the seacock looked OK, the badly dezincified tail pipe split. A second problem was that the Crash Test Boat has lost weight recently, so the outlet was above the waterline. To ensure we got some flow, we removed the bungs in the two drain holes and flooded the boat to an inch over the sole boards, then asked the travel hoist operator to raise the stern and roll her slightly to port to get the outlet under the water. Once we had flow, we started the test.

For our first test, we knocked out the log impeller with a hammer, breaking the fitting at its top edge

1. Using a hammer, Paul smashed the transducer fitting to hull level

2. The cracked toilet outlet tailpipe left an irregular hole to block

3. We even used a potato which formed a perfect seal to stop the leak

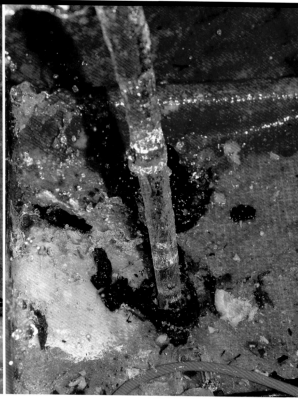

The result was an impressive leak – if ever you've removed your log or depth transducer you'll be familiar with this leak

Next we smashed the fitting away at hull level, leaving a hole that gushed a column of water

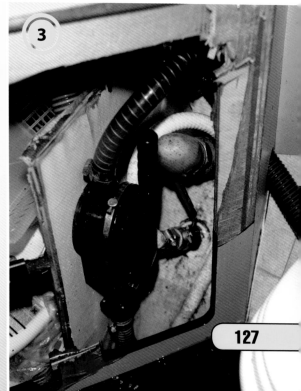

REAL LIFE STORY

1. *A new ¾ inch DZR engine raw water intake lost its outer flange*
2. *This brand new ½ inch raw water intake seacock for the galley sink broke off in Jonathan's hand – it had lost the entire outer flange and half the threaded area and was only held on by Sikaflex sealant under the internal flange!*

How a failed seacock could sink your yacht

Stray electrical currents in marinas, or from your own boat, can corrode your seacocks with potentially disastrous results

When yachtsman Jonathan Markovitz (pictured above) fitted a new Beta 25 engine on his Vancouver 27, *Seachord*, he did most of the installation work himself and got an engineer to check everything before signing off the warranty. He then connected the seacock and hull-anode bonding wire to the engine block. Two weeks later, returning from his first weekend cruise of the season from Hamble, the 70-amp hour engine starting battery was flat. It was five years old, so Jonathan assumed it was dead and replaced it as a matter of course.

Two weeks later, on a long weekend cruise to Poole Harbour, he discovered the new engine battery's voltage was very low. He started the engine from the domestic battery bank using car jump start leads. 'The warning signs were that the domestic battery bank seemed to be draining, too,' he said.

Sailing back to Hamble, he was so concerned he stopped at Lymington and asked marine electrician Andy Newport to check what was going on. Andy discovered the seacock bonding wire was connected to the starter-motor positive instead of being earthed to the engine block! 'I was tired when I did this and it proved to be a very expensive mistake,' said Jonathan with hindsight. The electrician reassured him that he was not the first person to have done this. The meter was reading 16 amps to the bonding circuit whenever the engine battery was switched on, whether the engine was running or not.

Jonathan immediately moved to the harbour wall, where he waited until after midnight to carry out a visual inspection of the hull exterior at low water. To his amazement he found that a brand new ¾ inch DZR engine raw water intake seacock had no outer flange at all. It was held in place just by the Sikaflex sealant on its inner flange. After spending the rest of the night on alternate seacock-watches he arranged an emergency lift-out first thing in the morning at Lymington Yacht Haven. Once the full extent of the severe consequences of stray electric currents

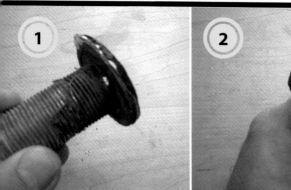

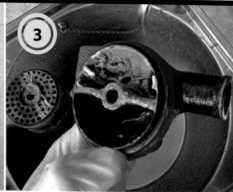

1. Different views of the same ½ inch galley seacock – badly corroded and weeping through the hole visible beneath the flange

2. This view shows the perforation on the screw threads on the inboard end of the seacock, with light is visible down the bore

3. The engine heat-exchanger – which had run for just 28 engine-hours since new, 24 of them with the faulty wiring – needed replacing. The anode had worn away and zinc deposits coated the unit

on a yacht's metal components were discovered, Jonathan ordered new seacocks from Aquafax which were fitted later that day. The bill, including haul-outs and a replacement battery, ran into hundreds of pounds. The only two seacocks that didn't seem affected were the heads sink outlet, which is on the waterline (it was cleaner than before but hadn't lost any structural material), and the cockpit drain seacock, which was not bonded.

Stray current corrosion happens when underwater metals are energised by an electrical current that has strayed from an electrical conductor or device powered by a battery, generator or dock power. It is the result of an electrical fault. Galvanic corrosion happens when two or more metals with different galvanic voltages are electrically connected and wetted by water. It is the result of the more active metal's natural tendency to give up electrical current to the less active metal. Galvanic corrosion can occur in fresh or salt water.

ARE YOUR THROUGH-HULL SEACOCK BOLTS SAFE?

Blakes bronze skin fittings are made of DZR (dezincifation- resistant brass), but the external plate could well be a tin bronze. The standard Blakes bolts should be phosphor bronze, a high strength version of tin bronze. Unfortunately, the bolts sold by the chandlery in this example were brass. After two years afloat, they had corroded badly.

LESSONS TO LEARN
by Vyv Cox, an expert in metallurgy

- If the live battery wire had been connected to any component on the negative side (e.g. engine block) a violent spark would have made it obvious something was incorrect. The bonding wire returned it back to negative and the resistance of the seawater was sufficient that no warning spark occurred.

- Stray electric currents, involving far less power than in this case, can be a problem for metals underwater. Direct and alternating currents, the latter in marinas with shore power connections, can accelerate corrosion.

- Jon's seacocks were bonded to the anode, and in this case to the positive terminal of the battery. Modern thinking, partially derived from the well publicised case of the Random Harvest near-sinking (see MAIB report on their website), is that bonding of skin fittings and seacocks is bad practice. All seacocks should be made from DZR brass, bronze, or another corrosion-resistant material then there is nothing to be gained by bonding or protection by an anode.

- Jonathan had softwood bungs attached to all his seacocks in case of failure. But if it happened on its mooring, with no one aboard, it would have been a different story.

As an experienced diver, Julio had no fear of jumping overboard to inspect the hull

How a coke bottle top saved a yacht from sinking

Spanish yachtsman, Julio Sanjuan, saved his 40ft motorsailer ketch, *Darwin*, from sinking after a seacock failure with an ingenious piece of improvisation. In July 2010, on a weekend sailing trip with his brother Antonio (51) and brother-in-law Pablo (46), they anchored in Cala Blanca, eight miles south of Denia, for lunch and a short siesta. He was asleep when Antonio woke him after discovering the bilge, a metre deep at its deepest point, was completely full. He tasted the water – in the past, the yacht's fresh water tank had leaked – but this time it was salty seawater.

The yacht had six bilge pumps, four electric and two manual. Two electric pumps were at the centre of the bilge and another in the stern, behind the engine. There was another big mobile bilge pump for emergencies. Julio's first reaction was to switch on the bilge pumps, before realising water covered two thirds of the engine, including the electric starter motor. It was impossible to start the engine. Luckily, the batteries were located at a higher level in special compartments, so the water still had to rise another 40cm to reach them. With the three main electrical bilge pumps they were able to stop the rising water, but they had to find a way to stop the leak.

The source, a seacock under the engine for the cooling water, was in an inaccessible location. Julio decided to dive under the hull to access the seacock outlet. They had to work together as fast as possible. Antonio was in charge of the emergency bilge pump, Pablo was responsible for checking the seacock and thinking about how to seal it.

Underwater photography is a passion for Julio so he didn't hesitate to jump in the warm Mediterranean water. Examining the hull, he could see the seacock's outer hull flange fitting had fallen to the seabed! In its place was a perfect circular hole. How could this happen? He also noticed the zinc anode on the prop shaft was missing.

They plugged the leak with some plastic bags before Julio remembered he had a special two-part underwater mastic for sealing holes. He prepared a ball about 3cm in diameter, but when he tried to plug the hole, the mastic couldn't withstand the water pressure. It was a race against time – the batteries would soon be discharged and the pumps would stop working, since they couldn't start the engine. Pablo realised the hole was the same size as the cap of a Coca-Cola bottle – his favourite drink! So Julio filled one of the caps with the mastic and tried again. Eureka! It filled the hole perfectly and the 'plug' stayed put. After four hours, they had saved the boat from sinking and managed to sail back to their berth at Denia Yacht Club with 28 knots of wind from the south-east.

Julio recommends inspecting your seacocks when the boat is laid up ashore. Take them apart and examine the components individually. In his case, the screw thread had disappeared, allowing the through-hull fitting to fall off. It was apparent that electrolytic corrosion had been going on for some time. The seacock was kept in place by the mastic sealant, but when as the yacht's hull was subject to movement for the first time in about four months, it simply fell out.

If you start using shore power aboard a boat that hasn't lived in a marina, get the bonding circuits checked. Also, beware 'stray current corrosion' caused by other boats. In Julio's case, a 50ft motorboat moored next to him was always connected to shore power. It may well have been 'parasite' current from this boat that caused the zinc anode on his prop shaft to drop off. As a result, the seacock became the sacrificial 'anode'.

Since the incident, Julio has taken various measures, including having an 'emergency sinking box', which contains plenty of underwater mastic, different types and sizes of plugs and caps. 'And I always carry at least two Coke bottles aboard *Darwin*, just in case!'

Antonio with the mobile bilge pump – just for emergencies

Pablo, with the Coke bottle that saved Darwin *from sinking*

7 FIRE

FIRE BLANKET

Guardian

How to fight a fire and how to prevent it

Fire is without doubt the most deadly disaster we had re-created thus far in the Crash Test series. A capsize or knockdown is dangerous, but its effects can be mitigated. Dismasting is a drama that doesn't always turn into a crisis. A hole in the hull, though a serious threat that could sink the boat, is an incident that might be managed with bilge pumps or any of the methods we tested. But when fire takes hold, smoke can be deadly and if the flames are beyond control, crew can be injured and the boat may be lost if the crew have to abandon her.

In 2010, RNLI lifeboats were launched in response to 120 fire incidents on boats and a total of 109 people were rescued. In 2009, there were 97 launches. The good news for yachtsmen is that in both years, only 28 of these incidents involved sailing yachts. Most call-outs were to motorboats, some with petrol engines. The RNLI's lifeboat crews, as a rule, focus on rescuing people and do not fight the fires themselves, although they are trained to deal with fire and have a simulator at Poole that puts them through their paces in a realistic (and hot) scenario.

Heat can be produced by a stove in the galley, an engine, a heater, a lamp, a candle, a cigarette, faulty electrical equipment, a short circuit

Every fire has three elements in common: heat, fuel and oxygen. If one of those elements is missing, a fire won't start. If one of those elements is removed, any fire can be extinguished

Electrical short-circuits, faulty appliances and power surges can start fires

and trapped or folded wiring. At sea it's generally windier than in port, so oxygen is abundant and we encourage its circulation. What about flammable material? Let's look at your boat. The hull is most likely GRP, which is glassfibre mat infused with flammable resin, the interior is probably wooden and the furnishings are foam and fabric.

Every cruising yacht is, in effect, a floating brazier, stuffed with material which will burn and shot through with ventilation holes. If a fire takes hold, few things will burn as well. Indeed, the fact that there aren't more catastrophic fires is testament to the general good practice yachtsmen exercise. The Boat Safety Scheme (www.boatsafetyscheme.com) states that, on average, there are 89 fire-related accidents and three fatalities each year on privately owned boats. Further research indicates that many of these are petrol fires on motorboats, but negligence can be fatal.

The aim of this test is to save the boat and crew. First, we'll look at firefighting, exploring how to fight fires on board, then we'll look at prevention.

A faulty dehumidifier set ablaze this Moody 54

' In 2010, RNLI lifeboats were launched in response to 120 fire incidents on boats and 109 people were rescued '

Fighting galley fires

Using paraffin as fuel, we started two different galley fires: one in a pan to simulate a fat fire and another using paraffin-soaked toast ignited on a stove-top toaster. We learned a lot from both tests.

Pan fire

Using an extinguisher on this type of fire risks blasting the burning oil all over the galley, spreading the fire and making it more difficult to tackle. Fire blankets are designed specifically to deal with pan fires but they need to be used correctly.

The correct method is to grasp the corners of one edge between thumb and fingers, palms up. Then raise your hands so the blanket touches the backs of your hands and turn your palms away so that the blanket wraps around your hands, protecting them. Next, making sure you keep the blanket between yourself and the fire. Lay the blanket over the pan, moving from inboard to out. This method doesn't cool the fire at all, so it's important to leave the blanket in place for at least 10 minutes, which allows the fire to lose heat. If you don't want to unpack your fire blanket to practise your technique, use a tea towel.

I was slightly concerned that the edge of the stove was higher than the pan, which meant the blanket would not necessarily prevent oxygen getting to the fire. In the event, I gingerly tucked it in and the flames, visible through the blanket, died out after a couple of seconds.

> **‘ Fire blankets are designed to deal with pan fires but need to be used correctly ’**

This blanket is mounted too close to the stove

Make sure you hold the blanket properly

Drape it carefully over the fire and step back

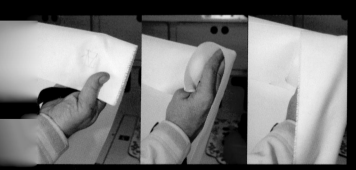

Holding the blanket like this makes sure your hands

Toast fire

We used a stove-top toaster and toast soaked in paraffin to start this fire. The plan was to use a foam extinguisher, then relight the fire and use a powder extinguisher.

A dribble from an untested foam extinguisher. Check your kit first

FOAM EXTINGUISHER
Firefighter Martin Lodge told me you should always shake and test an extinguisher before using it in anger. Give it a quick blast to make sure it works. I grabbed the boat's foam extinguisher, pulled out the safety pin, pressed the trigger and a dribble of brownish water issued forth. This showed the importance of testing an extinguisher and the need to keep all your safety equipment serviced, in-date and ready for use. Safety kit that doesn't work is worse than useless – it's dangerous. Had I attempted to fight a fire with this extinguisher, not only would I have endangered myself needlessly, I would also have lost seconds that could be decisive in the battle to get the fire under control.

Martin handed me his foam extinguisher and the paraffin-soaked toast was lit. There was an arc of foam but it wasn't hosing out with the force I'd expected. I kept waiting for the pressure to build and establish a jet of foam but it never did; that's not how foam extinguishers work. Inside the canister, firing the trigger releases a foaming agent that mixes with water to form the foam. The foam then forms a layer on the fire denying it oxygen and extinguishing the blaze. Martin also pointed out that I was standing too close to the fire. Although the pressure of the foam jet was anti-climactic, it was strong enough to knock one of the slices down the back of the stove, where it continued to burn. After extinguishing the fire on top, I sprayed foam below the stove and the fire was out, but it was an object lesson in how easily fires can spread if fought clumsily.

With the curtains in jeopardy, it's time to use the foam extinguisher

I stood too close and the foam blew burning toast off the stove

With a piece of burning toast behind the stove the fire wasn't out yet

Powder extinguisher

The powder extinguisher, used on the second toast fire, was far more impressive. It jetted out in a white mist which obscured vision and coated everything with white dust. It was possible to see the burning toast for a couple of seconds but then a huge cloud enveloped the saloon and I was hosing blindly. Powder is non-toxic but it gets into the eyes and crunches between the teeth in an unpleasant way so, once the fire was extinguished Martin ushered me into the cockpit. He pointed out that, if you're absolutely certain a fire has been extinguished, you can disable the extinguisher by holding it upside down and firing it – the gas escapes but not the powder. This stops somebody else trying to fight a blaze with used equipment.

Standing further back, the powder provided a more impressive blast

Fighting engine fires

We had planned two engine room fires. The first was to be extinguished by Sea-Fire Europe's FG100M automatic system, which uses the Halon replacement gas FM200. The second fire was to be fought with a 4kg powder extinguisher with a hose aimed through the hole we cut into the companionway steps.

AUTOMATIC SYSTEM

The first fire was set using paraffin in a metal pot under the engine. The automatic extinguishing system triggers when the temperature inside the engine room reaches 70°C, before electrical insulation wire or piping starts to burn. As backup, the automatic system had an external manual trigger so that it could be fired should the temperature not reach the required level for automatic firing.

Once the fire was set and the engine bay closed, there was a notable change in the smell and amount of smoke. After about 30 seconds, Martin, who had previously expressed concerns about the Crash Boat's 30-year-old engine soundproofing (the accumulation of flammable oil deposits on its foam surface), as well as the security of its attachment, instructed Sea-Fire's representative, Malcolm McIlveen, to trigger the system manually.

Once triggered, the FM200 should be left in its enclosed space for 10 minutes to continue its cooling effect. However, a minute later the fire was clearly still alight so Martin took steps to fight the fire directly, using the foam fire hose through a hole we had previously cut away in the cockpit liferaft locker (for just such an emergency), above the engine.

Sea-Fire Europe's FG100M automatic system has a temperature-sensing head that fires at 70°C

Within a second, the source of the fire is no longer visible...

... and within two seconds, you can't see anything. You're fighting blind

As the engine room fire gets out of control, the firefighters step in

We then removed the companionway steps and used carbon dioxide. It took three firefighters about 10 minutes to extinguish the blaze which filled the saloon with choking black smoke.

Analysing the engine fire later, Richard Duckworth, Sea-Fire's business development manager, summed up his thoughts on what had happened.

'The paraffin fire was rapidly put out by the FM200. However, due to the general poor state of the engine room – not surprising, considering what the boat had been through – the soundproofing collapsed over the engine and its flammable underside ignited. This, combined with the sudden inrush of oxygen when the companionway steps were opened, could well have led to the fire taking hold again. At this stage, the concentration of FM200 would have been too low to extinguish the fire.'

' The soundproofing collapsed over the engine and its oily underside ignited '

Engine fire out of control...

It took three firefighters 10 minutes to save the boat

Fire-retardant soundproofing fell off the bulkheads. Its flammable reverse burned

Martin inspects the fire-damaged soundproofing that fell on the engine

Manual method

Understandably, Martin was reluctant to start a second engine room fire, with concerns that the first could possibly re-ignite, so our second 'firefight', a powder extinguisher through a hole, was a bit one-sided.

1. A hose is essential for this type of engine firefighting

2. Powder covers the engine. It will enter air intakes too

The effects of smoke

To demonstrate how quickly a fire can take hold and how much smoke is generated, Martin and his team set a paraffin fire in a small frying pan on the galley stove. Needless to say, the Crash Test Boat's galley isn't used. There are no tea towels on the stove rail, no dish cloths, no handy kitchen roll, no matches, olive oil or tin foil – none of the flammable materials one might expect to find in the average galley.

The fire burned for 2 minutes and 40 seconds before Martin and his team decided the deckhead was in danger of catching fire, creating a blaze that could destroy the boat. In that time, the curtains above the stove caught fire and there was heavy charring to the wood veneer inside the coachroof. In the event of a fire, you should close all hatches to limit the oxygen reaching the fire. We needed ventilation to clear smoke so that we could film and photograph the test. With all the hatches closed, visibility would have been zero with a cloud of thick, black, acrid smoke and oxygen levels would have been very low. Without breathing apparatus, the firefighters would undoubtedly have been overcome.

In many ways, smoke is the most dangerous element in a fire. How do you fight a fire if you can neither see nor breathe? All you can do is get off the boat, alert emergency services and wait for the inevitable.

Charring was clear. She would be lost if the deckhead caught fire

1. The paraffin fire is set
2. The air is soon unbreathable
3. It's extinguished using CO_2
4. A pall of smoke remained

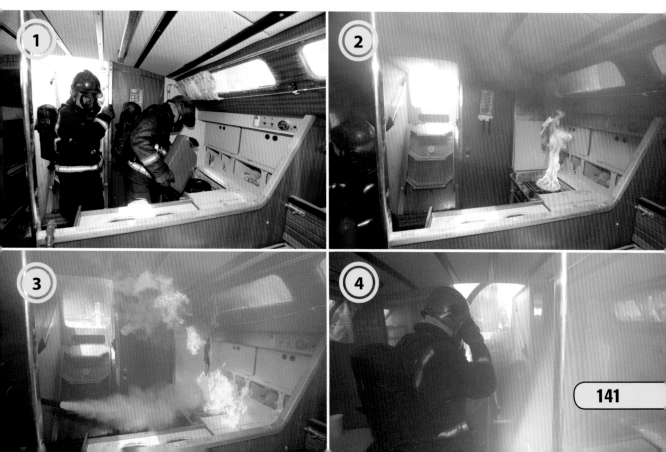

What we learned

We started this test hoping to learn how to fight fires, how to prevent them getting hold or out of control – or starting at all. It would be easy for you to read the lessons we learned and file it under 'I'll get around to it', but be under no illusion: without Martin and his firefighting team, we would have lost the Crash Test Boat. Indeed, Martin warned us that if the fire did get out of control, the best option would be to sink the boat rather than risk the fire spreading to the pontoon.

' Without Martin and his team we would have lost the Crash Test Boat '

Firefighting tips

• Send a Mayday
Fire seriously endangers boat and crew, so have no qualms at all about sending a Mayday distress call. It can always be cancelled once the fire is dealt under control or extinguished.

• Forget the mess
Dry powder makes a mess but fire makes a bigger one. You can't see anything once the powder has been discharged. It's unpleasant, but it's non-toxic and can be cleaned up. Fire and smoke will kill you, powder won't.

• Curiosity kills
A fire blanket or powder will kill a fire by removing oxygen. It doesn't remove fuel or heat, so always wait for at least 10 minutes after the fire is extinguished before inspecting the scene. Reintroducing oxygen could restart the fire, as it seems to have done during our test.

• Think it through
Position firefighting equipment where it's accessible. Don't put a fire blanket above the stove or even in the galley, and always have a fire extinguisher mounted in a cockpit locker. Engine or galley fires could prevent you from going below.

• One hand for the ship
Ideally, choose an extinguisher that can be used one-handed. At sea, you will need one hand to steady yourself while firefighting.

• Keep your distance
Stand well back from a fire: 2m (6ft) at least, and fight from as low a position as you can. Standing too close means the pressure from a fire extinguisher could spread the fire as well as exposing you to flame, smoke and powder. Fighting from a lower position keeps you out of the worst of the smoke and clear of any fireballs, like the one we saw when extinguishing the last galley fire.

• Worse than useless
Keep all extinguishers regularly serviced. You may never use them but if you need to, they must be charged and in working order. If I'd had to fight a fire with the feeble dribble produced by the Crash Test Boat's foam extinguisher, I would have lost the battle and put myself in considerable danger.

Prevention

GET ALARMED

Fit smoke, gas and carbon monoxide (CO) alarms and test them regularly. For the engine room fire we were hoping to test the Flame Spotter, an alarm system that alerts you to the presence of flames over 25mm high in two or three seconds. It 'spotted' a cigarette lighter flame in a preliminary test and the UK's lifeboats have had them fitted for a decade. However, after nearly losing our Crash Test Boat in the first engine fire, we took Martin's advice and abandoned a second test.

Install smoke, gas and CO₂ alarms. They don't cost much and save lives

PUT IT OUT

Never leave any flame or very hot item unattended – including stoves, candles, soldering irons, etc.

Make regular checks of all your systems, including gas

MAINTENANCE

Maintain fuel, engine, electrical and gas systems regularly and thoroughly, and regularly inspect sound-proofing for cleanliness and secure attachment.

Make sure your engine bay is sealed and that the soundproofing is flame-retardant and securely attached. Make sure there are no wires running over the top of the engine.

AUTOMATIC EXTINGUISHING

Seriously consider an automatic system in the engine bay. If you decide not to, make sure there's a firefighting hole in the companionway, with a cover you can remove and replace, and a powder extinguisher with a hose nearby. Opening the engine bay feeds a fire with oxygen and will make it worse, but you can investigate smoke using the firefighting hole as an inspection hatch.

Our 1982 boat had no firefighting hole for the engine. Make sure yours does

HOW ACCESSIBLE IS YOUR FUEL SHUT-OFF?

Make sure you can cut off fuel and gas supplies from the cockpit. Going down below might not be an option. We discovered that the Crash Test Boat doesn't have a fuel shut-off switch at all. Had we not taken the advised precautions, the engine fire could have shattered the primary fuel filter's glass bowl and left the diesel fuel tank emptying into the engine bay, literally adding fuel to the fire.

Which extinguisher do I need?

There are six types of fire extinguisher available for marine use, but different fires call for different extinguishers.

Fire type	
Class A	(Solid: wood, paper, fabric)
Class B	(Liquid: diesel, petrol, white spirit)
Class C	(Gas: propane, butane)
Class D	(Metals: sodium, magnesium, potassium)
Class E	(Electrical)
Class F	(Fat)

Extinguisher type	Fire type
Water	Class A
Foam/AFFF	Classes A, B, F
Powder	Class A, B, C, E
Carbon dioxide	Classes B, E, F
Fire blanket	Class F
FM200	Class A, B, E

CARBON DIOXIDE
Carbon dioxide extinguishers work by preventing oxygen getting to the blaze, but take care not to blast the fire from too close, which could spread the flames. Used in a confined space, suffocation or unconsciousness is a risk.

WATER
Water extinguishes fires by neutralising heat. It can only be used on Class A fires, so it probably doesn't justify a place on board. A bucket over the side would work just as well and it's cheaper.

POWDER
Powder is the most multipurpose extinguisher. It coats the fuel, denying it oxygen, but it doesn't cool the blaze so reignition is a possibility if the fire is disturbed.

FIRE BLANKET
A fire blanket works by preventing oxygen getting to the blaze, so extinguishing the fire. It's important that the blanket covers the pan completely, to prevent oxygen reaching the fire.

FOAM
Foam, or AFFF (aqueous film-forming foam), is water mixed with a foaming agent. The foam spreads over the fire and denies it oxygen, thus extinguishing it, but it doesn't cool the blaze.

FM200
Halon (L), in the green extinguisher, is now illegal in the UK and other parts of the world, due to the damaging effect the fire extinguishing agent has on the Earth's ozone layer. Use instead FM200, pictured in the red extinguisher.

What size do I need?

Powder extinguishers are measured in kilograms, reflecting the weight of the powder, and foam extinguishers are measured in litres of stored pressure volume. A 2kg powder extinguisher (around £30) will give you about 7 seconds of firefighting, a reasonably long time for anything but an engine fire. Prices for 2-litre foam extinguishers start at around £20.

How we did the test

We wanted to start fires in the galley and engine room and extinguish them using the boat's existing equipment, all of which was out-of-date and needed servicing. To gain an insight into the dangers involved, we decided not to use special fire-retardant clothing, gloves or eye protection. Like every other yachtsman in this situation, I was wearing nothing more protective than oilskins.

Having completed a merchant seaman's firefighting course in the 1980s, I was well aware of the dangers – not just flames and the rate of spread, but the effects of toxic smoke on visibility and respiration. Our consultants on the test were professional firefighters from the International Fire Training Centre at Warsash Maritime Academy: Martin Lodge, Andy Baynham and Barry Marsh, in full firefighting gear, with breathing apparatus. An emergency fire hose was rigged down the pontoon with an engine-driven pump siphoning seawater.

The Crash Test Boat had one fire blanket and four fire extinguishers: a 1 litre foam extinguisher dated 2005 and kept in the galley, and three 2kg powder extinguishers, all dated 2006, one in each of the cabins. We decided to use those for the galley fires. None was suitable for the engine room fire because none had a hose that could be pushed through the firefighting hole in the companionway steps. In fact, the yacht, built in 1982, had no hole pre-drilled through the steps, so we drilled one. Ocean Safety supplied us with some recently out-of-date 2kg powder extinguishers, one of which had a hose attached, and a brand-new 4kg powder extinguisher, also with a hose.

The International Firefighting Training College prepares to set fire to the Crash Test Boat

(L–R) Firefighters Andy Baynham, Sub-Officer Martin Lodge and Barry Marsh

We made two safety modifications to the Crash Test Boat. Osmotech drilled a 5cm (2in) hole in the companionway steps for an extinguisher hose and a 7.5cm (3in) hole in the bottom of the cockpit floor liferaft locker, above the engine, for a fire hose. The diesel tank was emptied and filled with water to prevent the build-up of vapour. Both fuel filters were removed and the engine oil was drawn off. The engine bay was cleaned and dried. Batteries were removed.

Sea-Fire Europe, which specialises in fire suppression technology, installed its automatic FM200 system for the engine room test. They tested a section of the engine bay's soundproofing and found it fire-retardant. However, its underside wasn't, and when the soundproofing fell off the engine room bulkheads, the fire burned on.

Fire in the Ionian

Derek and Carol Asquith's charter holiday got off to a hair-raising start when they were called to rescue the crew of a burning yacht

It was the second day of our flotilla sailing holiday in the Northern Ionian. The winds were light, the sea was flat and the sun was shining as we left Mourtos for Parga. The fleet was a mix of 9.7m (32ft) Jeanneau and 11m (36ft) Beneteau yachts and my wife, Carol, and I who sail a 7.3m (24ft) Snapdragon at home in North Wales, had looked forward to the comfort of as larger boat for the holiday.

We sailed between the Sivota Islands and the mainland, cruising slowly down the coast. After a couple of hours the wind died completely so we started the engine. The sea was calm as we motored at a comfortable 4 knots towards the next headland in the distance. We noticed the lead boat close inshore three or four miles ahead of us, with only one or two boats of the flotilla in sight.

Suddenly the radio came to life with one of our group calling the lead boat in a fairly calm way saying they had a fire. We turned the volume up and scanned the horizon but could no signs of smoke anywhere. Our lead boat responded on the VHF channel the flotilla was using, asking if they had found the source of the fire and made any effort to extinguish it. They replied that the fire was in the engine compartment and one extinguisher had made no difference.

The lead skipper then asked their position and from their reply we realised they were perhaps half a mile ahead of us with no one else around. The flotilla lead skipper then told them not, on any account, to open up the engine compartment, but to try to use the second extinguisher through the hole in the companionway steps panel. After some tense moments they came back to say that their efforts with the second extinguisher had proved unsuccessful.

At this stage, I called the lead skipper to tell him we were closing with the boat. We increased speed towards now visible smoking yacht and saw four men

waving frantically and more smoke pouring from the cabin. When we were within about 25 metres we could hear them shouting. 'Hurry up, it's going to blow!' Carol turned to me and quietly asked if I thought it would really explode. I crossed my fingers and replied confidently: 'Diesel won't explode, it will only burn.' Pulling alongside the stricken yacht, we found three crew amidships and one standing in the pulpit, as far from the smoke and burning as possible. Carol held a fender over the side to prevent the lifelines becoming entangled as we came alongside in the swell. We did not want to be trapped against a burning yacht, even for a few seconds.

The three men amidships scrambled aboard, calling for the fourth in the pulpit. In his panic, the fourth man jumped overboard into the sea. We veered slowly away and Carol threw a fender to the man in the water who could not swim as fast as the boat. She then took a mooring warp from the cockpit locker and we reversed very slowly until she could throw him the line. With the engine in neutral we pulled him towards the bathing platform and after a successful recovery motored clear to take stock of the situation.

The crew of the blazing vessel were all wearing T-shirts and shorts and had only two lifejackets between them as the others were stowed below in cabin lockers which were impossible to reach because of the fire. Carol made them hot coffee, gave the wet crew member a towel and a large sweater, and called the lead boat to inform them that we had transferred the crew.

The lead boat arrived a short while later, but by now the fire had really got hold and no one could have safely gone back aboard.

As we watched, the shrouds gave way and the mast collapsed and fell into the sea. Soon the gas bottles exploded in the cockpit and that was the beginning

REAL LIFE STORY

of the end. The lead boat later tried to tow the hull but, when it became obvious she was sinking, they took her back to deep water where she soon went down.

As we returned the four crew to Mourtos, they told us that, as with all the flotilla boats, they had a liferaft and inflatable dinghy; but since no one had been given instructions in launching the liferaft, they had failed to inflate it. They had tried to pump up the dinghy, but felt it was taking too long and had given up. No doubt the proximity of our boat had led them to feel they had more chance of escape with us. Luckily, all survived unharmed.

LESSONS LEARNED
We instantly moved our lifejackets from the cabin into the cockpit lockers and made sure we knew everything we needed to about out how to launch the liferaft.

It was our first real man-overboard and, although the stern bathing platform is considered the wrong place from which to recover a person, on an almost flat calm day the platform with a ladder made it easy.

Should you be unfortunate enough to have engine fire aboard, throw the gas bottles and any spare fuel cans overboard to prevent them exploding. A longer lead on the VHF microphone and a hand-held set in the cockpit would have helped. Apparently, the cabin of the blazing yacht filled with black smoke so quickly that it was soon impossible to go below.

I intend to fit bigger extinguishers on our Snapdragon, including one in a cockpit locker. And to make sure than anyone who comes aboard has a thorough safety briefing and knows where everything is stowed and how it is operated.

Derek and Carol Asquith started sailing in 1984 together in dinghies in North Wales.They bought their Snapdragon in 1993 and cruise as often as they can during the summer from, Conwy to the Menai Strait and the Llyn peninsula, as well as to Ireland.

(Extract from Total Loss, edited by Paul Gelder, Adlard Coles Nautical)

8 EXPLOSION

How safe is your gas system?

The Crash Test Team created a deadly gas leak to show why gas safety and regular checks are so vital.

This final dramatic test in our eight-month long Crash Test Boat series was carried out with serious reservations and concerns, not to mention trepidation. In all our previous trials – including capsize, sinking and fire – we experimented with various ways of coping with emergencies so we could tell readers from first-hand experience which one worked best. But a gas explosion is in a different league. It's unpredictable and there are no half measures. You either survive or you don't.

We asked the Marine Accident Investigation Board (MAIB) for details of recent cases where gas bottles were involved in explosions and fires on leisure craft. Steven Clinch, the Chief Inspector of Marine Accidents, gave us a dossier with 18 reported incidents 'of interest', most of them within the last 10 years. Many involve motorboats and canal boats, but they also include sailing boat incidents, one resulting in a known fatality. A huge percentage of gas leak 'incidents' are not reported unless they involve the emergency services. We know of other incidents abroad that have also not been reported in the UK.

How our boat became a floating time bomb

Unless you have witnessed first-hand the destruction caused by a gas explosion, it's difficult to comprehend the aftermath.

We enlisted the help of the Royal Navy's Fleet Explosives experts, from Navy Command HQ in Portsmouth, for this, the most technically challenging and complex trial in our Crash Test Boat series. David Stopard, an expert in gas installations on yachts, was also our consultant.

The site chosen for our test was off Bembridge Ledge, at the eastern end of the Isle of Wight, where the yacht was anchored in 8m and a 200m exclusion zone was set up under the watchful eye of the Queen's Harbourmaster at Portsmouth. On hand to set up the detonation of the blast was RN Fleet Explosives Staff Officer Lieutenant Commander Harry Palmer, with Petty Officer Simon ('Frank') Spencer.

The first attempt failed, after a suspenseful 25-minute wait for the gas to disperse in the yacht's cabin and mix with oxygen. On the second attempt, a simplified method was used to ensure the crucial gas-air mix. A split second after detonation by a wireless remote 'trigger' from the Navy's RIB, there was a brief orange fireball followed by the explosion. A hundred pieces of GRP debris were hurled skywards amidst a plume of smoke.

Minutes later, the Crash Test Boat Team sped to the wreck in two RIBs. Gruesomely floating in the water was an 'amputated' leg from one of the Crash Test dummies, complete with sailing boot. Next we recovered the torso, cut in half and still wearing its red oilskin jacket. The dummy had been placed standing in the cockpit beside the companionway.

As we came alongside, the scale of the carnage was clear. The entire coachroof had been blasted off the hull and seemed to have disappeared. We later recovered it half-submerged and still attached to

David explains the system to the Royal Navy's Petty Officer Spencer

the jury rigged mast stump which hung over the starboard side.

Despite sealing the saloon doors with gaffer tape to confine the gas to the saloon, the blast wave had extended right through the yacht, from bow to stern. It had blown open the anchor locker and blasted the hinges off the cockpit lazarette. The granny bars had been twisted into some morbid modernist sculpture.

Windows had been blown out and the foredeck had buckled and split along the centreline and become detached completely from the hull on the starboard side. Analysis of film footage and photographs reveals that the foredeck was very nearly blown off the boat. Its starboard edge is shown at an angle of 30 degrees to the hull and fixed to the boat only by the bow roller. Its aft edge was a flange of torn GRP trimmed with the deck's balsa core. Further aft on the starboard side a second split from coachroof to toerail had sliced clean through the starboard genoa track. As the mast of our jury rig had rocketed upwards in the explosion, its Dyneema 'shroud', lashed to the toerail, had refused to give way and ripped off the toerail, now a piece of mangled scrap.

A scene of devastation

Climbing onboard, amidst the wreckage of jagged glassfibre and torn metal, the sense of danger and insecurity was palpable. Stanchions and guardwires had been snapped off in the blast like twigs and garden twine. The hull-deck joint had split asunder, and even the knees, which had connected the sidedecks to the hull, had been blown away. Without support, the sidedecks threatened to collapse as we crawled on deck on our hands and knees.

The cockpit was the only recognisable structure left more or less intact. Where the deck had lifted, the bridgedeck had splits either side of the companionway. The engine room bulkheads held the cockpit in place. The starboard locker lid had been blown off, exposing the distorted aft bulkhead, which had been blasted backwards and was now wedged in the locker.

Looking ahead, into what was left of the saloon, nothing was where it should be, save for the saloon table – with the two gas bottles which had caused the devastation, still intact and taped in position – and the chart table and galley. The galley sinks were blasted out of their wooden frames and lay upside down. Lockers had been blown open, the companionway steps displaced. Sections of deckhead and sole littered the interior. The doors to the aft cabins were blown in and the forehatch was missing.

Epicentre of the blast

On reflection, it was not surprising that the saloon table was the least damaged area as it was at the epicentre of the blast, the point from which the shockwave emanated. We were surprised that the Crash Test dummy, positioned next to the chart table and now half buried in the wreckage, displayed no signs of shrapnel damage or scorching – there were no holes in its oilies and it hadn't moved a great distance. I was astonished to see most of the bulkheads remained in place.

The blast shatters the deck and distorts the hull – but she stays afloat

The blast filmed by a remote video camera in the cockpit

Anatomy of a gas explosion

A gas explosion has two elements: blast effect and 'flame event'. The blast effect is the mixture of fuel and air detonating in much the same way it does in the cylinder heads of an internal combustion engine, causing a rapid expansion in volume. This sudden expansion creates the shockwave that causes structural damage, punching through the deck and smashing the interior.

The blast effect is accompanied by a 'fireball' as the gas ignites. It reaches about 3,000°C but lasts less than a fifth of a second, as revealed by Yachting TV's cameras, shooting at 25 frames per second. Wood burns at 450°C, so the flame was too short-lived to set fire to the yacht's furnishings below. We had removed much flammable material before the test, including engine oil, diesel and distress flares, as part of a careful risk assessment.

153

1

2

3

1. The scene immediately after the explosion when it was feared the yacht might be sinking
2. Chris Beeson in the wrecked saloon. Nothing was where it should be, save for the saloon table
3. The Crash Test dummy lies crushed amongst the wreckage of the galley with the twin sinks blasted upside-down
4. Paul Gelder and Chris Beeson survey the wreckage
5. Devastation, with the aft cabin door blasted into the chart table area, exposing the ensuite heads
6. The coachroof and broken mast section hanging off the bow
7. The force of the blast split asunder the hull-deck joint along 80% of the yacht's length

Gas safety checklist – 7 essentials

David Stopard, an expert in gas safety, offers seven vital safety checks plus six tips on what to do and what not to do if you smell gas aboard your yacht

1 HAVE IT CHECKED BY AN EXPERT
Safe gas installation is essential. Ideally, you should have your system inspected and tested by a GAS SAFE-registered engineer. Some say it should be done annually.

2 FIT A GAS LEAK DETECTOR
Install a bubble leak detector which is fitted in the pipe downstream of the gas regulator. To test for leaks, shut off gas appliances and press the button. Gas flow is diverted through a bowl of glycerin and bubbles reveal an unsafe leak.

3 SAFE INSTALLATION
Never stow gas bottles outside the airtight gas locker. They can and do leak. Always stow them upright and make sure they are securely strapped into place. It is never a good idea to stow gas bottles alongside flammables, like this outboard engine petrol tank.

4 ALWAYS SWITCH OFF
Always turn off the gas at the bottle when you have finished using it. Before you leave the boat, always check the gas locker to make sure the supply is turned off and the regulator is securely attached. In the *Lord Trenchard* accident (see page 162), the gas locker was not gas-tight and gas leaked into the yacht's main hull with deadly consequences.

5 CHECK YOUR SYSTEM
Carry out a visual check of the gas system every time your visit your boat. There are plenty of warning signs of danger. Is your gas pipe chafed? Do you have armoured hose?

6 TURN OFF GAS FIRST IN A FIRE
Make sure you have a fire extinguisher and a fire blanket for galley fires. If a fire breaks out in the galley, turn off the gas first, using the shut-off valve. As soon as you can, turn it off at the bottle, too.

7 A GAS LEAK ALARM IS ESSENTIAL
Install a good quality gas leak detector, making sure the sensor is at the boat's lowest point – probably down in the bilge. The sensor needs to be waterproof. There are tri-detectors on the market that can detect gas, carbon monoxide and smoke, but you might want to fit smoke detectors in each cabin, too, as fires tend to happen where there are people.

reasons to double-check – real-life disasters

Marine Accident Investigation Branch reports of incidents of explosions or fires involving gas bottles, show that in many cases a gas detection system was not in use or failed to work

How safe are thousands of boats used around the UK that have not had a Gas Safe Registered check? Many yachts have had poor DIY work carried out, says gas expert David Stopard. Is your system safe and when was it last checked?

2004 A fire and explosion was caused when the crew of a boat were changing gas cylinders with candles alight in the cabin. The vessel was declared a total loss.

2005 The deck of a 22ft sloop, berthed in Emsworth, West Sussex, was blown off and the owner later died in hospital. Multiple explosions were caused by gas and an outboard petrol tank that ignited.

2005 A fire on a sailing yacht on passage for three days was thought to have been caused by a gas leak. A gas detector on board had not gone off during the incident. Two crew abandoned ship and were rescued from their liferaft.

2006 A suspected gas leak on a motorboat in Brighton Marina resulted in the owner suffering serious burns.

2007 An explosion on a boat in Scotland was caused by a leak in the gas pipework to the stove. Two crew suffering burns had to swim ashore. One died later in hospital.

2007 A gas explosion on a boat in Norfolk was thought to be caused by a loose gas hose on the cooker ignited by a spark from an electric bilge pump or fridge compressor.

2007 A sailing boat in Pwllheli was declared a total loss following an explosion while the boat was moored in the harbour. The source of ignition was thought to be a Calor gas powered refrigerator. The owner was badly burned but his wife was luckily sitting in the cockpit. Both were taken to hospital.

2007 A Cornish Shrimper on the Norfolk Broads suffered a small explosion when a camping stove being used in the cockpit was not properly turned off after boiling a kettle. The accumulated gas leak caused an explosion and minor burns to the crew.

What to do if you smell a gas leak

1 Don't panic. Your nose is very sensitive and gas alarms detect leaks at very low levels. A mixture of 2–9% of gas to air is needed to cause an explosion.

2 Shut all gas cylinder valves to stop any more gas escaping.

3 Turn off gas appliances, electrical equipment and your engine. Don't switch off the battery bank because that will turn off your alarm, plus VHF radio, GPS and nav lights, which you may need. It may seem obvious, but don't look for gas leaks with a naked flame.

4 Ventilate the boat by opening all hatches, windows and lockers. Lift the sole boards if you can without risking sparks – don't use an electric screwdriver if they're screwed down.

5 Manual bilge pumps can only shift around a cubic litre per stroke and there are several thousand litres of air mixed with gas in your saloon. It's quicker to grab the washboard and waft air towards the companionway. Turn on the gas alarm occasionally to see if it still detects gas.

6 Don't use the gas system again – even if the alarm has stopped and you can no longer smell gas. Get it checked by a Gas Safe engineer.

How we blew up the Crash Test Boat

An orange flash and a loud bang signalled the successful conclusion to hours of planning meetings, phone calls and emails when the Crash Test Boat exploded. How did we do it?

'There's a fair chance the yacht won't survive,' said the Royal Navy's Fleet Explosives Staff Officer, Lt Cdr Harry Palmer. 'We only want to do this once!' he added. 'I'll be surprised if the deck is left on!' was the prescient verdict from Peter Spreadborough, of Southampton Calor Gas Centre Ltd (SoCal).

Like most of our Crash Test Boat experiments, the results were not predictable. The two worst-case scenarios were complete failure to trigger an explosion, or creating such a big bang that the yacht sank. Owner, Robert Holbrook, MD of Admiral Insurance, confirmed we were covered for 'removal of wreck'. We had a salvage vessel from H Attrill & Sons Ltd, one of the oldest boatbuilders on the Isle of Wight, standing by with a pump and lifting gear.

To create a gas explosion you need a mixture of 2–9% of gas to air. We sealed the saloon from the rest of the accommodation so we were dealing with a known volume, calculated at 18,900 cubic litres. Too much gas, or too little, and the 'brew' is unlikely to detonate.

Gas safety experts, David Stopard of Marine Systems Engineering, and Peter Spreadborough, decided to use two 465g propane canisters, containing a total of 517 litres of gas, a mere 2.7% of cabin volume.

A plan was devised by Stopard with Kevin Stockwell of Nereus Alarms to deliver the gas into the yacht in a controlled manner.

David Stopard set up the gas canisters in a plastic supermarket basket in the cockpit. The gas was fed into the saloon via a long orange rubber gas pipe. When this method failed we tried plan 'B'

Bottom left: PO Spencer installs flash igniters

Bottom right: Second time round the gas canisters are turned upside down and the valves opened to prevent freezing

The Royal Navy's radio-controlled detonation signal was sent by wireless remote (see photo right) to a control box on a float on the yacht's deck

After 30 minutes with no alarm, Lt Cdr Palmer gives the order to fire but nothing happens

The gas cylinders, placed in a basket in the cockpit, would feed gas into the yacht's saloon via a long hose. A small electric computer fan on the saloon floor helped to mix gas and air. A Nereus alarm system was fitted with two pre-calibrated LPG sensors. A high-pitched alarm would activate when the gas-air mix reached an explosive level (5%). If detonation failed, a solenoid switch would shut off the gas and switch on two fans to disperse gas through the hatchway. A second alarm, with a low-pitched noise, would sound the all-clear when it was safe to go aboard. Everything was powered by a sealed motorcycle battery in the cockpit.

> ' *We sealed the saloon so we were dealing with a known volume of gas in the yacht* '

The plan was approved at a meeting at the Royal Navy's Command HQ in Portsmouth, by Lt Cdr Harry Palmer and Michael Archer, Diving and Explosive Ordnance Disposal Officer. The Navy would take charge of detonation using military grade 'flash igniters' (a sort of 'electronic matchstick,' said Harry). They would be triggered by radio signal from a Navy RIB sent to a control box mounted on a buoyant float on the deck of the Crash Test Boat.

David tested the theory outside his workshop, filling a small cardboard box with gas. When the high level alarm sounded, he lit the gas with a Piezo igniter. Singed eyebrows were proof of success!

'I realised we had to half-open the gas bottles to stop them freezing up, which meant the saloon would take 25 minutes to reach ignition level,' he added.

Chris Attrill's salvage vessel recovers the coachroof which was blasted off

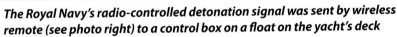

'It was the nautical equivalent of shock and awe,' said Paul Gelder

First time unlucky

It was a case of 'will the last man on board turn on the gas'. LPG was piped into the saloon and dispersed through a drilled copper pipe attached to the deckhead to give the best chance of mixing with air. Royal Navy Petty Officer Diver Simon Spencer installed several flash igniters around the pipe which would be triggered simultaneously. The system was primed and we retired beyond the 200m exclusion zone.

After a tense 25 minutes no alarm sounded. We decided to attempt ignition anyway. The countdown '3-2-1… fire' was followed by silence. Ten seconds later, smoke was seen wafting out of the hatchway. 'Puff of smoke but no cigar!' was David's verdict.

Without waiting for the 'all-clear' alarm, Lt Cdr Harry Palmer took the Navy RIB towards the yacht with David Stopard onboard. 'I turned off the gas cylinders and PO Spencer put out a small fire in the saloon with a

dry powder extinguisher,' said David. The fans were switched on to disperse smoke and powder.

Failure was thought to be due to three factors: the gas cylinders had partially frozen, slowing gas flow. A gap in the washboards allowed too much ventilation. The flash igniters weren't low enough.

For the second attempt David mounted the canisters lower down. They were turned upside down so the gas left the bottle as a liquid, which soon evaporated into a white cloud of vapour. No more freezing problems. PO Spencer rigged new igniters and the system was primed again. The companionway hatch was closed and taped up. After a couple of minutes, the high level alarm sounded and we all retired the full 200m, near the RNLI's Tamar class lifeboat. This time it took just five minutes before the command to detonate was given. It was the nautical equivalent of shock and awe.

The last journey home

She's been called 'the unluckiest boat in the world'. The valiant Crash Test Boat's final, poignant voyage afloat was under tow with Sea Start. With lone skipper Chris Beeson on the helm, the main concern was whether the towing bridle would tear off the deck, which was no longer joined to the hull or bulkheads on the starboard side.

Fortunately, the remaining bulkheads left her with enough rigidity to ride the Solent chop without the hull crumpling. The yacht safely arrived back at MDL's Hamble Point Marina, though her new 'cabriolet' configuration did take in some water from spray.

The deck remained with hull but the new sunroof let in some spray

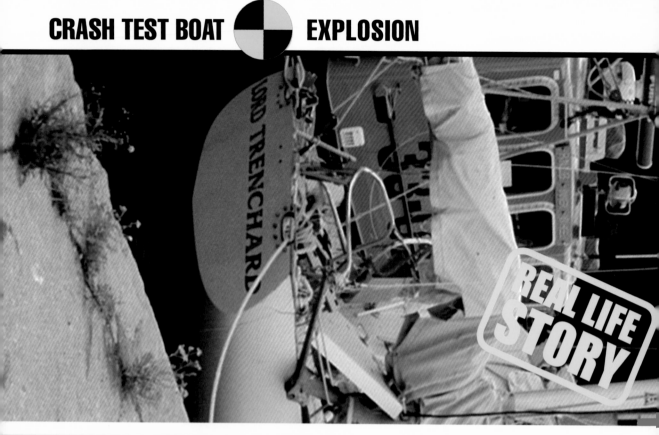

REAL LIFE STORY

A disaster waiting to happen

Gavin McLaren was first mate on *Lord Trenchard*, a 55ft Nicholson yawl belonging to the Joint Services Adventure Sail Training Centre, which suffered a gas explosion in Poole Harbour at 0710 on 30 June 1999. Skipper Colin Rouse was seriously injured. Gavin's first-hand account of the accident makes sobering reading for anyone with a gas system aboard their yacht

The sound of people moving around the cabin and quiet conversation wakes me. It is broad daylight and I glance at my watch. Five to seven – I can doze in the quarter berth for a few more minutes. I pull the bunk curtain aside just in time to see two of the crew disappear up the companionway with their shower gear. The skipper, Colin Rouse, is up and about. 'What's the weather like?' I ask.

'Fine,' he answers. 'Looks good for Cherbourg. Kettle's on.' I lie back and think about the plan for the day. Seven crew members will be joining us after breakfast and in my mind I run through the briefing that they will need before we can sail. I hear the generator, fitted below the cockpit, turn over as Colin tries to start it from the control panel by the saloon steps. It doesn't start the first time and then I hear it turn over again.

Chaos. I am conscious of the most excruciating pain. The whole of my right leg feels as though it is being electrocuted. The agony goes on and on and on. I can't see, I'm covered in something white and translucent. There is no noise, and then I hear screaming. Deep male cries of agony; it takes a finite time for me to realise that the screaming is coming from me. Illogically, I think that something must have happened to the generator and live cables have dropped across my leg. After what seems like an age the pain starts to ease.

Faintly I hear a voice. 'He's lost his leg'. I turn my head to the right and see a severed leg lying beside my bunk where the chart table seat should be. For one dreadful, heart-stopping moment I think that it's mine. Then I realise that the leg is deeply tanned and wearing a shoe and sock – it can't be me.

I think I lose consciousness at this point and the next thing I am aware of is someone dragging me from the remnants of the quarter berth. They are pulling shattered sheets of glassfibre off me. I am lying on the bare hull, the bunk has disappeared from under me. My rescuers drag me through the gaping hole where the coachroof had been. There is a stink of glassfibre, as though I was in a moulding shop. My face and eyes are covered in blood and something seems to have happened to my right foot – it's bleeding and won't take my weight. I look back into the wreckage of what had been the saloon.

Colin is lying there with people working on him. The stump of his leg is pointing straight towards me. The cabin is devastated – I cannot conceive what has happened. There is blood everywhere.

I recall nothing else until I step onto the jetty from TS *Royalist*, alongside which *Lord Trenchard* had been berthed. There are police cars and ambulances all over the quay and more are arriving. I only hear their sirens faintly. There is a lot of broken glass and a crowd is beginning to form, held back by the police. A sergeant is talking to me, but I can't really absorb what he is saying. He shakes my shoulders. 'How many people were on board. How many?' I try to pull myself together. 'Four!' I answer.

I look back at *Lord Trenchard*. The whole of the cockpit and aft deck has disappeared, leaving a gaping hole some 20ft long. The mizzen mast has fallen forward and the aft end of the coachroof has been torn off. I can see a deep split running down the hull from the coaming to the waterline. The whole deck has been lifted and all the windows blown out. Only at this moment does my mind register what has happened – explosion. I want to go back to the boat to help Colin but, sensibly, I'm not allowed to. 'He's all right – he's being looked after,' I am told.

Still dripping blood, I am put into an ambulance and driven away. That is the reality of a gas explosion. The violence of the event is beyond belief. The blast was heard over four miles away and windows blown out on the quay, despite being shielded by the bulk of *Royalist* inboard of *Lord Trenchard*. The other two crew

members on board, who had, like me, been lying in their bunks, were miraculously uninjured, but very shocked. The two crewmen who had just stepped onto the jetty probably saved Colin's life. They recall looking round to see parts of the boat – including the complete wheel and binnacle – flying high in the air. They came back on board and administered first aid, helped by officers from *Royalist*, until medical help arrived.

The emergency services deserve every praise. Poole lifeboat came alongside and together with *Royalist* supported *Lord Trenchard* to keep her afloat; she was making a lot of water from the splits in the hull and damaged seawater systems. After Colin had been taken ashore she was towed to the other side of the harbour to be lifted out. I spent some time in casualty, together with members of *Royalist's* crew, who had suffered cuts and bruises. I had the gashes in my foot stitched up – the cuts to my face were only superficial – and discovered that both my eardrums had burst.

The initial pain in my leg, which had been only a few inches from the seat of the blast, was explained to me; the shock of the explosion had stimulated all the nerves in it at once, a common blast effect.

Whilst being treated I heard that Colin's left leg had been amputated above the knee. His other leg was badly damaged but had mercifully been saved. He also had injuries to his hand and neck and, although critically ill, was out of immediate danger.

Later that day I went back down to *Lord Trenchard* to try to retrieve some of my personal kit. She was still being kept afloat, but was half full of water and diesel fuel. The interior was almost unrecognisable with virtually nothing left intact. The explosion had obviously happened under the cockpit and the blast had torn forward through the boat, ripping out the joinery, bulkheads and cabin sole. The forehatch, which had been secured with a massive wooden strongback, had been torn off. The chart table had been blown forward through the saloon, together with the radar and all the instruments.

It seemed impossible that four people could have survived. Mixed in with the shattered fragments of

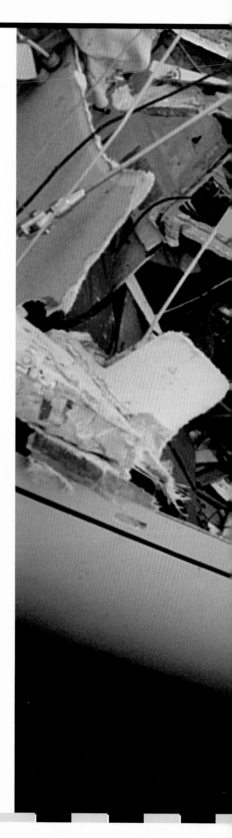

glassfibre and plywood were the pathetic remains of personal possessions – shredded clothing and sleeping bags, books, toilet gear, Colin's battered flute. It was a very shocking sight, made worse by the evidence of Colin's injuries – splashes of blood and blood-soaked clothing.

How could such an accident happen? The Joint Services Adventurous Sail Training centre in Gosport had been running a fleet of 24 boats, including nine Nicholson 55s, for nearly 30 years. The boats were deployed world-wide – three of them were racing across the Indian Ocean when this accident happened. They have a regular programme of refits and maintenance and, because many of the service personnel who sail in them are novices, safety procedures and routines are paramount. The Marine Accident Investigation Board carried out a very thorough enquiry into the explosion on behalf of the Health and Safety Executive.

Like the other service Nicholson 55s, *Lord Trenchard's* gas system consisted of two 3.9kg propane cylinders, mounted in a gas locker sunk into the deck abreast the cockpit. Both cylinders were connected by flexible hoses to the regulator via a wall block and from there a single continuous gas pipe ran to an isolating valve by the cooker. A retaining plate secured the cylinders in the locker with just their shut off valves exposed. One cylinder was turned on whilst the other, shut off, was a standby, available when the in-use cylinder ran out. Whenever the cooker was not in use the isolating valve beside it was kept shut. A gas alarm was fitted, with two sensors, one beneath the cooker and one below the cockpit.

The evening before the accident the in-use gas bottle ran out whilst supper was being cooked. It was turned off, the standby cylinder was turned on and a note made to change the empty cylinder next day. The accident report identified three failures that caused the explosion. First, the standby cylinder, which had been turned on the previous evening, had not been properly connected to its flexible pipe. The cylinder was recovered after the event and the connection was loose. It had been attached during a previous cruise made by *Lord Trenchard* a fortnight earlier and had been the 'standby' cylinder since then. Thus, when, twelve hours before the explosion, this cylinder was turned on, high-pressure gas leaked undetected directly from the bottle into the gas locker.

This gas should have drained overboard. However, examination of the gas locker, which was also recovered, revealed that it was not completely gas tight. So an unknown proportion of the escaping gas leaked into the watertight compartment below the cockpit. The final cause of the disaster was that the gas alarm failed to operate. The reason for this could not be determined – the alarm system was so badly damaged in the explosion that testing it was impossible. The report concluded that the generator starter motor supplied the spark that ignited the gas.

(Extract from **Total Loss**, *edited by Paul Gelder, Adlard Coles Nautical)*

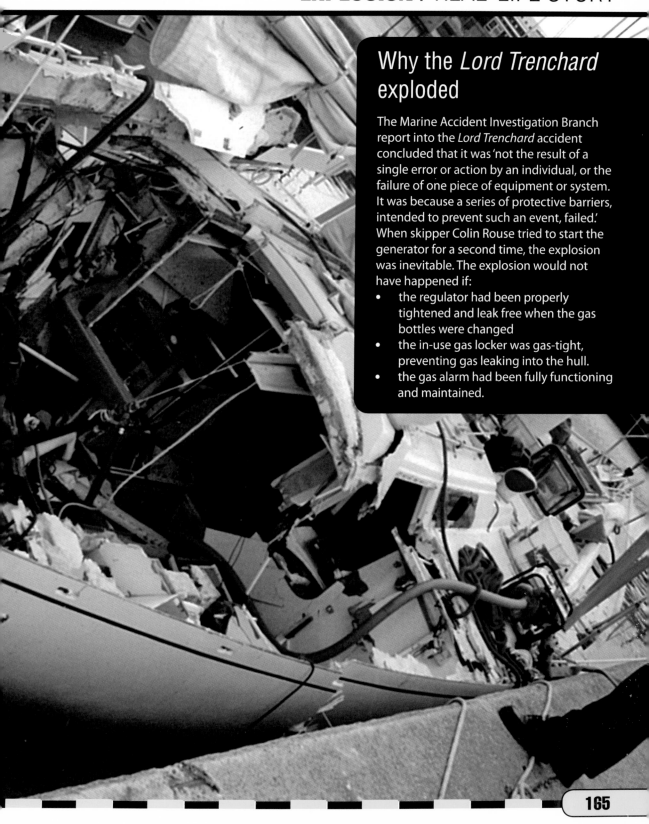

Why the *Lord Trenchard* exploded

The Marine Accident Investigation Branch report into the *Lord Trenchard* accident concluded that it was 'not the result of a single error or action by an individual, or the failure of one piece of equipment or system. It was because a series of protective barriers, intended to prevent such an event, failed.' When skipper Colin Rouse tried to start the generator for a second time, the explosion was inevitable. The explosion would not have happened if:

- the regulator had been properly tightened and leak free when the gas bottles were changed
- the in-use gas locker was gas-tight, preventing gas leaking into the hull.
- the gas alarm had been fully functioning and maintained.

Filming the Crash Test dramas

Steve Adams recalls the challenges of filming fire, capsize, explosion and sinking in the Crash Test Boat series

When I was approached to film the Crash Test Boat series, by Paul Gelder, then editor of *Yachting Monthly*, I knew it would be one of the most difficult technical challenges I'd ever faced. But it would also be one of the most relevant film series made for leisure sailors.

My first assignment was the 360° capsize test in Ocean Village Marina. Filming from inside the boat was too dangerous. Instead, I used two remote Minicams, the type of camera used by the BBC's Natural History unit in situations when it's too dangerous for a cameraman.

I've used many different cameras over the years but the recent emergence of remote GoPro HD cameras has opened up new possibilities. I placed two GoPros in waterproof housings and clamped them either end of the saloon. When the boat was upside down, it would be very dark inside so I used portable battery spotlights. The resulting graphic footage revealed the horrors of loose items which became deadly flying 'missiles'. With hindsight, I would have liked to build a rig that allowed the cameras to rotate as the boat heeled.

The second test – Dismasted – was, potentially, one of the most hazardous, filmed in winds gusting 30 knots-plus. When the mast came down, the rigging wires could whiplash like giant cheese cutters. I filmed from behind the helmsman, but next to the backstay! I installed two remote GoPro cameras – one on the bow pulpit and another on the stern to capture the action. I concentrated on looking down the lens and put my trust in skipper Paul Lees, from Crusader Sails. I never thought I'd feel so pleased to see a mast go over the side.

For the sinking test, a hole was smashed in the forward section of the hull and we cut away some of the bulkheads so I had space to film. It was unnerving when we took on two tonnes of water in seven minutes as the yacht was lowered into the water in MDL's travelhoist. At times like this, you focus on looking through the viewfinder and leave the worrying to the rest of the team!

The GoPro cameras also came into their own with the fire test, allowing me to get close to the flames without putting myself in danger. To get the main shots I lay on the coachroof and lowered the camera through the coachroof hatch. If the heat or smoke got too much I could escape. In fact, it did many times and I was shocked at the speed with which the smoke affected all of us.

Steve has been bringing sailing to our screens with Yachtingtv.co.uk for 5 years

Steve adjusts one of the two HD remote cameras that filmed the capsize

Steve Adams at the heart of the action with Crash Test Boat skipper Chris Beeson and Royal Navy explosives expert

The dramatic finale to the series – Explosion – produced the ultimate test. How to film the event without destroying equipment worth hundreds of pounds? Once again, I used the trusty GoPro cameras – one inside the saloon and another clamped to the wheel support in the cockpit. The cameras were in waterproof housings, but I had no idea how the explosion's pressure wave would affect them. Both GoPros survived the blast. The cockpit camera captured incredible footage as the coachroof blasted off. The saloon camera captured the moment of detonation but the screen went white in the explosion's flash. I found it buried under layers of debris. I was filming from outside the 200 metre exclusion zone. A 10-9-8 countown always makes the heart beat faster. I remember just concentrating on keeping the boat in the middle of the frame and holding my breath as I watched the boat explode in the viewfinder.

YM's Crash Test Boat series has been a major technical challenge. It's been a privilege to work with the Crash Team, but I may just hesitate next time they invite me for a sail!

Steve Adams is a keen sailor and professional film-maker. He has worked for Meridian TV, the Travel Channel and Sky TV. In 2007 he launched Yachting TV, an online sailing video magazine. His longest assignment was crossing an ocean with the Atlantic Rally for Cruisers in 2007. www.yachtingtv.co.uk

'You were only supposed to blow the bloody doors off!' exclaims Robert Holbrook as he inspects his yacht

The exploded hull-to-deck joint

Aftermath of the explosion

The sense of relief following the safe conclusion of the most dangerous and potentially costly of all our destructive tests was palpable. But even when the yacht was back at Hamble Point Marina, there were concerns about the integrity of the hull. With bulkheads blown out, would it break like an eggshell when the crane lifted her ashore, squeezed by the slings and unsupported by water pressure?

Surveyor, Edward Sawyer: 'The yacht expanded like a balloon in the explosion'

I invited yacht surveyor Edward W Sawyer to check the yacht's structural condition before we prepared her for display to the public. Edward had recently been involved in an insurance claim on another yacht that had suffered a serious gas explosion in the Mediterranean. The skipper and his wife were aboard – in the cockpit – at the time of the incident and were lucky to escape with their lives. Their yacht had been declared a total loss, but the owner was so fond of her that, at great expense, he had her transported back to the

UK where a new deck was made and fitted, and other major repairs carried out.

In both explosions the damage was very similar. Edward noted that internally some 50–60% of the Crash Test Boat's bulkheads and partitions had been 'profoundly damaged' and that virtually all the bonding and tabbing to cabin partitions and locker bulkheads had detached from the hull. The hull-to-deck joint had blown apart on the starboard side from the bow along 80% of the yacht's length and 50% on the port side. The explosive pressure had blown out bulkheads at the aft end of the two aft cabins and there was evidence of 'escape routes for rapidly expanding gases', such as the blowing out of hatches, windows etc.

Viewing our slow-motion video recording of the explosion, Edward noted that, as he suspected from the Mediterranean yacht's damage, 'the craft had expanded momentarily, like a balloon, before the pressure was suddenly released. For the most part, this let the hull moulding return to its normal shape, with the deck and coachroof moulding suffering all the dramatic damage. In the video and photos you can actually see the entire deck lifting up 40 degrees or so and then viciously snapping back into place.

'The shockwave or pressure wave from an explosion can do weird things,' I had been told by the Royal Navy's explosives expert. A survivor of the 7/7 terrorist bombings in London in 2005 sitting on a bus very close to the bomber suffered perforated eardrums,

broken teeth and cuts and bruises, while 13 other passengers died. The gas canisters that wreaked such havoc on our yacht on the Crash Boat amazingly remained pristine and untouched by the blast.

The Crash Boat was built more than 30 years ago in a traditional GRP building style. Many people have speculated how a modern production

At the seat of the blast the gas canisters remained untouched by the blast

yacht, relying on internal module mouldings – often secured with flexible sealants/adhesives – to provide the structure, would withstand such a blast.

On a reassuring note, Edward concluded that yachtsman should not be unduly concerned about the use of LPG on their boat (provided it is properly installed and maintained) because, in his view, 'it is proven to be by far the safest of the fuels available if handled correctly.' He added: 'I've been to more fires started in galleys through the use of liquid fuel cooking devices than from butane/propane.'

The YM crew on Fizzical at Southampton Boat Show: front row (left to right) Dick Durham, Chris Beeson and Paul Gelder. Back row: Graham Snook, Rob Peake and Andrew Brook

Shipwreck showcased

It was always part of the grand plan to exhibit the Crash Test Boat at the UK's two biggest boat shows – assuming she wasn't lying at the bottom of the Solent – as a 'wake-up call' for yachtsmen to witness first-hand the consequences of poor maintenance and encourage self-reliance and good seamanship.

Although she had been set ablaze just a few weeks before Southampton Boat Show, the yacht was still afloat, though the engine was kaput, with all the electrics destroyed, so she had to be towed up Southampton Water to the show's marina.

Originally, National Boat Shows planned to position our battered, scorched wreck beside the 'Try-a-boat' feature. But when it was pointed out that this might frighten off show-goers, rather than encourage them to take up sailing, they reconsidered. The yacht was on display more appropriately opposite the RNLI lifeboat.

Photo credit: onEdition

Richard Shead, our marketing manager, spent a small fortune on air-fresheners to try to disguise the aroma of charred wood, plus the musty scent of damp upholstery from the capsize and 'sinking' tests. Down below, everything in the galley area was coated in a layer of white powder from the fire extinguishers.

Yachting Monthly's youngest crew member, Andrew Brook, was aboard throughout the show, but was instructed not to allow general members of the public down below. I didn't want to fill out any more risk assessment forms, or face any accident claims.

The yacht's final public appearance was scheduled for the Tullett Prebon London Boat Show from 6–15 January 2012, where she would be visited by HRH Princess Anne and her husband, Vice Admiral Sir Timothy Laurence.

After the gas explosion, the boat desperately needed heavy-duty cleaning before being fit for public display. Despite putting a protective cover over the gaping hole where once there had been a coachroof, strong winds, combined with the jagged splinters of GRP, shredded our attempts to keep out rainwater. Holes were drilled in the bottom of the hull and furniture to drain away gallons of water lying in pockets in the bilges, as well as drawers and lockers.

Richard Shead, in charge of our boat show stand, was concerned not just about the post-explosion smell, but feared leaks from inaccessible parts of the hull

The biggest clean-up challenge of Richard Houghton's life

when the boat was exhibited lying on her side so people could look into the shattered cabin. I wrote to Richard Houghton, an enthusiastic fan of the Crash Test series, who runs his own company, Yacht Charter Ltd, and asked: 'How would you like the biggest cleaning challenge of your life?'

Richard, whose armoury includes industrial vacuum cleaners and a jet wash, wrote back: 'It seems a shame to sterilise the visual impact of such a work of twisted destruction! I think the shock and awe of seeing what's left in all its shattered resin-blasted goriness

The Crash Test Boat arrives at the ExCel Exhibition Centre

would hold great appeal for the disaster voyeurs among us!'

Truth was, there was so much wreckage in the saloon, we couldn't move, let alone drain all the water without removing some of it. And cushions and other material had to be dried out.

Transporting the wreck from Hamble to the ExCel Exhibition Centre in London's docklands was another challenge. PSP Worldwide Logistics had shipped yachts for Dee Caffari, Bear Grylls and Sir Robin Knox-Johnston, so we were relieved when they agreed to organise the Crash Test Boat's penultimate 'voyage' along the M25 free of charge.

The boat was transported with an escort as a 'Convoi Exceptionnel' and Jo Dixie, PSP's PR and Marketing Manager, arranged for Wild Graphics to make a 15ft sticker to go down both sides of the hull bearing the message: 'We'll take care of your boat – not wreck it!'

Together with Crash Test Skipper Chris Beeson, Richard Shead and *YM* photographer Graham Snook, I was at ExCel for the boat's arrival three days before Christmas. After a seven-hour wait for a crane she was unloaded from the low-loader and, with the aid of two fork-lift trucks, manoeuvered into place amidst some ghastly creaking and crunching of GRP. 'Careful, don't scratch the hull!' joked the workers, who were more used to handling polished showcase yachts. It was a 'first' for the British Marine Federation and National Boat Shows to have a 'capsized' shipwreck displayed at one of their shows. It helped that they gave us free space, regarding the project as education as well as 'a show-stopper'!

The wreck was to form part of the biggest stand IPC Marine Media had ever had at a boat show – conveniently next to the Black & White Guinness Bar, where show-goers could gawp at their worst nightmare and enjoy a pint. To add to the scary scene, Richard imaginatively 'dressed' the stage set with some of our Crash Test dummies hanging out of the shattered hull, and added a smoke machine and a flashing red light to make the most of the macabre atmosphere.

Head of marketing Richard Shead, who masterminded the boat show display, pictured with Paul Gelder. Below: a smoke machine and flashing lights added to the macabre atmosphere at ExCeL, where the shipwreck was a show-stopper. Photo credits: Terry Beasley

Royal seal of approval

Princess Anne, a keen sailor herself, took one look at the smoking hulk and asked: 'What should one do about gas safety?' Her husband said: 'I always turn off the gas at the bottle as soon as we've finished with it.' Had they, I wondered, heard the story told by former *YM* editor Des Sleightholme, who was driving home from his boat one weekend and asked his wife, Joyce: 'Did you turn off the gas?'

'Yes, of course!' she said.

'So did I!' replied Des.

The Princess and Vice Admiral laughed.

When I explained that the two Royal Navy experts who assisted us during the explosion were Lieutenant Commander Harry Palmer (nothing to do with *The Ipcress File*) and Petty Officer Diver 'Frank' Spencer (nothing to do with the BBC's accident-prone comedy, *Some Mothers Do 'Ave 'Em*) there were more smiles from the couple who were soon to take delivery of a new Rustler 44.

Princess Anne and her husband, Vice Admiral Sir Timothy Lawrence, both keen sailors, visited the Crash Test Boat. Photo credits: onEdition

Robert Holbrook meets the Princess

The royal seal of approval was a wonderful culmination following months of hard work by the Crash Test Team and our army of behind-the-scenes helpers. We celebrated at the show's late night opening with a Shipwreck Party – 'at your own risk', of course – on the stand. Tongue-in-cheek invitations were sent to industry VIPs and all our sponsors. The dress code was: 'Fireproof, waterproof, or survival suit. No lounge suits or reefer jackets.'

The boat show also saw the launch of *Yachting Monthly*'s iPad App of the Crash Test Boat series, which combined text, photographs and video footage of the eight disasters, plus podcasts and inter-active content. Many people had written to *Yachting Monthly* asking 'What's happening to the boat when you've finished destroying her? Can I have the old winches, binnacle compass, wheel etc?' Others had wondered how we would dispose of a wreck beyond economic repair.

Paul Stevens (left) is using the Crash Test Boat to teach a new generation of yacht surveyors

Alas, she was already 'spoken for'. Paul Stevens, part our Crash Test Team, had been running a hands-on Practical Yacht & Small Craft Surveying Course at the International Boatbuilding Training College, in Oulton Broad, Suffolk, and wanted to use the Crash Test Boat as a teaching aid. In what would become the nautical equivalent of an anatomy class for medical students,

his pupils would practise their skills on the wreck of *Fizzical* and learn what signs to look for after accident damage, or how to spot attempts to hide damage or make poor repairs. The unique course was entering its sixth year as we went to press, with delegates from all over the world.

The International Sailing Federation (ISAF), the world governing body for the sport of sailing, is also using the Crash Test Boat project to promote offshore safety awareness and training among its 137 member nations. Henry Thorpe, Co-ordinator of the Technical and Offshore Department of the ISAF Secretariat, said: 'It's been a great project to follow.' So even in her after-life, the Crash Test Boat continues to teach us and is educating the yacht surveyors of tomorrow.

There will never be such a thing as a disaster-proof yacht. But if the Crash Test Boat project has encouraged sailors to become more 'disaster-proof' themselves and made them think more deeply about safety-at-sea it will have accomplished what we set out to achieve. Like all good Hollywood disaster movies, will there be a Crash Test Boat 2? More than 30 years after our boat was built, it would certainly be interesting to know how a modern assembly-line-built production yacht would withstand the sort of tests ours endured.

Last voyage for the Crash Test Boat as she makes 'landfall' at the International Boat Building Training College in Suffolk. Photo credit: John Richardson

Thanks to all our sponsors who made all these tests possible

CRUSADER SAILS

Admiral ·BOAT INSURANCE·

MDL Marinas

OCEAN SAFETY

ROYAL NAVY

Lifeboats

PSP WORLDWIDE BOAT TRANSPORTATION

Yachting TV
Sail & Power in Vision

RYA

Nereus Alarms ltd

WARSASH MARITIME ACADEMY

Marine Systems Engineering

OSMOTECH UK
YACHT REPAIR AND RESTORATION

Gill

THE WILD GROUP

PSP SOUTHAMPTON BOAT SHOW

LONDON INTERNATIONAL BOAT SHOW AT ExCeL LONDON

tullett prebon

SEA START
MEMBERSHIP

Mike Golding Yacht Racing

Acknowledgements

Unlike a Hollywood disaster movie we had no cast of thousands, but we did have a veritable army of indispensible behind-the-scenes helpers. Nothing like this had ever been done before and we were all out of our comfort zones.

As *Yachting Monthly*'s editor, I ultimately carried the can for the success or failure of the Crash Test project, but more than once I have been credited, wrongly, with what a rival sailing magazine blogger called 'a gloriously inspired, insufferably good idea!'

There is, they say, no such thing as an original idea. In the 1970s YM editor Des Sleightholme launched 'The Troubleshooters', in which a series of yachting disasters were created to test the resourcefulness of eight volunteer readers. Bill Anderson, then RYA Cruising Secretary, was an observer and describes how Des, after passing his Yachtmaster exam, thought about the many practical skills he had never been tested on – exercises deemed too risky, costly or time-consuming to stage. Des set up a series of realistic disasters – running aground, abandoning ship, leaving crews offshore in liferafts – to see how they coped. Crews were also dumped offshore in mastless keelboats, and told to improvise jury rigs from an assortment of spars, sails, wire and rope. There was an invitation to an end-of-cruise supper in Salcombe – if they could get there!

In the last 30 years many editors have tried to resurrect the idea. But the 'light bulb' moment that projected the Crash Test Boat idea into a new, more daring, ambitious dimension was getting hold of a yacht we could test to destruction. 'How about asking an insurance company to supply it?' said YM's art editor, Simon Fevyer.

It was pure serendipity that Robert Holbrook, boss of Admiral Yacht Insurance, was looking for a sponsorship opportunity at the time. Thanks to Abigail Hatter, from Creative Media at IPC Inspire, and Adam Fiander, who runs a marine PR and

marketing company, a meeting was set up. It's a testament to Robert's unwavering belief in the project and his bravery in backing what some derided as 'a crazy, journalistic stunt', that we were able to achieve success. If Robert had any doubts or fears that a real-life accident might tarnish the entire project – let alone our reputations – he kept them to himself. Robert introduced me to Jim Hirst and Mike Ingram, founders of Osmotech UK, a top yacht repair company, who sourced a 40ft Jeanneau yacht at a bargain price – and repaired her between disasters. Chris Beeson, skipper of the Crash Test Boat, did a great deal of pre-test research and lead the team on the water, as well as writing the in-depth test reports. Having lived through, and survived, all the re-created disasters, he soon became adept at coping with panic situations. Staff photographer Graham Snook also worked closely with Chris on the set-up and execution of tests and did a great deal of work on storyboarding the iPad 'App' for the Crash Test Boat. Chief photographer Lester McCarthy also had invaluable input.

Keeping a watchful eye on proceedings was Stephen Gates, IPC Media's Risk Manager, together with insurance advisor David Lanfranchi, from Marsh & Mclennan Companies, and Tony Bodycombe, a health and safety expert, who checked our risk assessments.

The RYA signed up as a project partner, with Cruising Manager Stuart Carruthers taking a keen interest throughout. Paul Boissier, CEO of the RNLI, gave his personal backing to the project, as well as an introduction to the Royal Navy for our explosion test. Peter Chennell, the RNLI's Sea Safety Manager, and Isla Reynolds, Public Relations Officer, also assisted. I cannot over-estimate how the RNLI's 'seal of approval' gave us the credibility we needed to open so many doors. John Eads, CEO at MDL Marinas, gave us free berthing and storage ashore, plus multiple crane lifts. Dean Smith, MDL's Marketing Director, and Hamble Point Marina Manager Mike Weldon and his team were all brilliant.

Apart from the Crash Test team listed at the front of this book, other individuals and companies vital to the project were Dave Kennett, former Yarmouth lifeboat coxswain, who skippered the salvage vessel during the dismasting. Peter Spreadborough, marine & leisure sales manager at Southampton Calor Gas Centre Ltd, introduced me to David ('Dave the Bang') Stopard, who masterminded the gas explosion. Chris Attrill, from H Attrill & Sons, helped us recover floating debris with his salvage vessel. Royal Navy Petty Officer Diver Simon (Frank) Spencer, Leading Diver Michael Swenson and Diver Stuart Ricketts also assisted at the gas explosion, as did Nick Hewitt, head boatman at Seaview Yacht Club. Steve Clinch, Chief Inspector of the Marine Accident Investigation Branch, provided statistics on gas explosions. Russell Gray, Principal Lecturer at Warsash Maritime Academy and Tom Johnson, Fire Team Leader at the International Fire Training Centre at the academy, helped set up the fire test. Charlie Mill, from Ocean Safety, Marlow Ropes, in East Sussex and Tetra Boats in Bristol, helped with equipment on various tests.

Nick Gill, Chairman and Founder at Douglas Gill International Ltd, donated oilskins for our Crash Test Dummies to wear in the capsize and explosion tests. When the Crash Test Boat was too damaged to sail or motor, Nick Eales and his team from SeaStart Ltd, towed us to and from Hamble Point Marina.

Greg Hoar, founder and Director of the Wild Group and Matt Straker, provided free graphics for our sponsors on the yacht, as well as graphics for the boat shows.

The British Marine Federation and National Boat Shows, through Marketing Executives Mike Enser and Ed Mockridge, gave the Crash Test Boat free exhibition space at Southampton and London Boat Shows. Richard Shead, Head of Marketing at IPC Marine Media, created a show-stopping display at ExCel Exhibition Centre. Thanks to Jo Dixie, PR and Marketing Manager for PSP Worldwide Logistics, and Gill Gould, the show went literally on the road when PSP transported our shipwreck to London Boat Show and, finally, her last resting place at the International Boatbuilding College, in Suffolk, where principal Nat Wilson and his wife Jill took over custodianship of the yacht.

Simon Owen, Publishing Director at IPC Marine Media, gave me enthusiastic support and wise counsel throughout the project. Thanks also to the authors of the real-life stories that accompany our 'created' disasters. Janet Murphy, Editorial Director and Jessica Cole, Senior Editor at Bloomsbury Publishing and Adlard Coles Nautical, plus Barry Pickthall and book designer Kayleigh Reynolds at PPL Design, all added their own invaluable ideas to the book which you are holding in your hand.